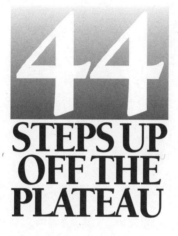

STEPS UP
OFF THE
PLATEAU

44

STEPS UP OFF THE PLATEAU

Lyle E. Schaller

Abingdon Press
Nashville

44 STEPS UP OFF THE PLATEAU

93 94 95 96 97 98 99 00 01 02—10 9 8 7 6 5 4 3 2 1

This book is printed on recycled, acid-free paper.

Library of Congress Cataloging-in-Publication Data

SCHALLER, LYLE E.
    44 steps up off the plateau / Lyle E. Schaller.
        p.   cm.
    Includes bibliographical references.
    ISBN 0-687-13291-6 (pbk. : alk. paper)
    1. Church growth. I. Title: Forty-four steps up off the plateau.
BV652.25.S32   1992
254' .5—dc20   92-23620
                                                                          CIP

MANUFACTURED IN THE UNITED STATES OF AMERICA

To

Allen

Dan

Dawn Susan

Susan Anne

Susan Leigh

CONTENTS

INTRODUCTION

Perhaps the most challenging undertaking for a leader in the church today is to go out and help plant a new congregation. This can be true for both the mission developer team as well as for those volunteer leaders enlisted by that three-to-five person team to help pioneer that new mission. (This also can be an unexpectedly lonely assignment for the minister who goes out alone to build that new mission.) One reason for the challenge is the absence of the momentum that has been built up in the long-established worshiping community. Another reason for this fascinating challenge is the absence of inherited traditions and customs that limit creative thinking. Part of the fun is in creating the new, in making order out of chaos, and in looking back and feeling good about what happened in such a brief period of time.[1]

Perhaps the most interesting assignment is to be a member of a leadership team in the large and numerically growing congregation that has been assigned the responsibility of creating a new specialized ministry. These teams usually include one or two paid staff members, plus several creative, dedicated, and enthusiastic volunteers who share a common vision. That vision may focus on expanding the missional outreach of that congregation, expanding the teaching ministry, feeding the hungry, nurturing children, planning a new worship service to reach a different slice of the population, serving developmentally disabled adults, strengthening the evangelistic outreach, or some other aspect of ministry. The central point is that everyone on the team has accepted this as a high personal priority and is eager to turn the vision into reality.

For many adult Christians the most comfortable assignment is to be part of a long-established worshiping community that is bound together by a common commitment to Jesus Christ as Lord and Savior, by meaningful friendship and kinship ties, and by a widely shared affection and respect for the current pastor. The cohesiveness of this community is reinforced by the power of local tradition, a common history, an attractive sacred meeting place, stability, predictability, and few surprises. The relatively slow pace of congregational life and the one-to-one relationships undergird that feeling of comfort.

Perhaps the most difficult assignment, for either a minister or a volunteer leader in the church, is to design and implement a strategy that will move the long-established congregation up off a plateau in size. That is the focus of this book. The reader should be forewarned that this is not a book filled with easy-to-implement formulas. Transforming the long-established church that has been on a plateau in size for years is an extremely difficult assignment! Why that is so often true is explained in the first chapter. It is increasingly difficult to devise a plan or a strategy or a course of action that will please everyone. This can be illustrated by the difficulty experienced by this writer's struggle to devise a sequential outline for this book.

Once upon a time, when everyone obeyed the laws of

the Creator, people would pick up a book and read it from cover to cover. Television has legitimized discontinuity. Today people turn from one channel to another without any feelings of guilt. Likewise many persons open a book and begin to read one chapter here and another there. This has complicated life for authors who prepare an outline on the assumption that (a) every reader will complete the first chapter before turning to the second chapter and (b) every reader will read the entire book.

In this world, which is populated by a growing number of liberated church members, voters, pastors, and readers, it may be impossible to design one action program that will please everyone. Likewise it may be unrealistic to hope to prepare an outline for a book that will make sense to every reader. Those who have read every word in every one of this writer's last two dozen books will find much that is familiar. Such a small crowd, however, can safely be ignored.

A far larger crowd includes those impatient activists who want to read only the chapter or two "that speak to my situation back home." This road map is designed for them. The impatient reader who is eager to undertake the radical changes necessary to transform the parish that has been on a plateau for years may want to turn first to chapter 10. Those who seek what is closest to a guaranteed formula may begin with chapter 4. Those who are confident that all we have to do is open the doors and invite people to come probably should seek a different hobby or transfer their membership to a rapidly growing congregation. Or they may want to begin with chapter 9. Those who are leaders in churches that have begun to grow up off that plateau in size and want to maintain that trend may turn first to chapter 11. Those who are deeply troubled by the fact that the consumer orientation is a growing trend may wish to skip chapter 10, which, in two different courses of action, affirms this shift from a producer perspective to a consumer orientation. That chapter may threaten the traditional view of how priorities and schedules are determined!

Denominational officials responsible for ministerial placement probably should concentrate on chapter 6. Those congregational leaders who want to choose from among a broad range of tested alternatives will find twenty-five choices in chapter 8. In that chapter, they can begin by choosing between seven steps filled with discontinuity with the past or eighteen that are less threatening.

The leaders from self-identified "small churches," averaging between 120 and 175 at worship, may find chapter 2 to be the best beginning point. Those who are convinced the prescription should be written after the diagnosis has been made will begin with chapter 3.

Those who have attempted to implement what they were convinced was an appropriate strategy, only to experience disappointing results, may want to begin with chapter 5 or the first half of chapter 12. For others, the barrier to the successful implementation of their carefully designed strategy is discussed in chapter 5. Not everyone is willing to pay the price of moving up off that plateau in size.

Ideally, many will discover that, with God's help, they were able to move their congregation up off that plateau, but they also discovered that success carries a price tag. That phenomenon is discussed in the last half of the last chapter.

All orthodox and patient Christians who love the Lord and who seek first to be faithful and obedient servants of the Lord will, of course, begin by reading this introduction and struggle through the succeeding chapters in the sequence in which they are presented.

At least a few of the less docile and obedient readers, however, may inquire about the motives for writing this volume when some of what is included here was discussed in greater detail in earlier books. This author's response is this book represents an effort to bring together in one volume a more comprehensive analysis of this difficult subject. The challenge to the leaders in the long-established congregation to move up off a plateau in size is far more difficult than it sounds. No one formula fits every church. No previous book discusses the variety of choices available to a broad range of churches. As the notes at the end suggest, a reader may want to turn to another source for a more comprehensive discussion of a particular point. That is the purpose of those notes.

Feedback from readers has revealed that this "44" series has attracted many people who enjoy counting, and several who can count beyond twenty. A few have built checklists to determine if the title represents misleading advertising. For their benefit this author's count declares one step up off that plateau is described in the second chapter, another is found in the third chapter, and the three most important are offered in the fourth chapter. Each of the next three chapters discusses a single step. Add those eight to the twenty-five choices offered in chapter 8, plus the six in chapter 9, and we have only five to go. Four of those remaining five are found in chapter 10. The last and most crucial step is described in chapter 11.

Now, dear reader, stop counting and start designing the strategy that will move your congregation up off a plateau in size. Counting can be useful, but do not let it be a substitute for planning and doing!

CHAPTER ONE

WHY? AND WHY NOT?

O ne reason I wanted to meet with you folks for a couple of hours before you begin your search for a new pastor is to talk with you about the rich potential of this congregation," explained a staff person from the regional judicatory while meeting with a group of volunteer leaders from Trinity Church on Tuesday evening. "You've just completed a five-year pastorate with a minister who has chosen to take early retirement. According to the material you submitted to our office, you've been averaging approximately 145 at worship and about 84 in Sunday school for the past several years. You've been receiving an average of fifteen new members annually, including five or six or seven young people from member families. Between 1980 and 1990 this community experienced a 50 percent net increase in population, and the experts are predicting an additional 60 percent increase during this decade. You're meeting in a good building on a five-acre site at an excellent location. We think that if you call the right pastor, you can more than double the size of this congregation. If you find the minister who would be the perfect match for the potential here, you might even triple in size in another dozen years. We would like to help you in that search for a new minister, since I expect you will all agree that choice will be the most influential decision you make this year."

"Who said we wanted to double or triple in size?" challenged Chris Becker, an influential member of the search committee. "Some of us believe we're about the ideal size for a church in today's world."

"I'm in favor of growth," commented another member, "but we've about decided the number-one quality we're looking for in our next pastor is someone who likes to visit. I don't want to sound critical, but I think our last minister was really too much of an introverted personality to be a pastor. He has a brilliant mind, and he is remarkably well read, but he prefers books to people. I think that's why he took early retirement. We have a lot of shut-ins and retirees who enjoy having a pastor drop in to visit. I believe if we can find a pastor who will visit, our people will come to church more regularly and our attendance will go up."

"I don't have anything against church growth," added another committee member, "but I don't think that's the most urgent issue. My wife and I have two teenagers, a thirteen-year-old and a sixteen-year-old, and I hope we can find a pastor who is good with youth. If you want an honest opinion, I don't think our last pastor knew how to relate to today's teenagers. I'm not blaming him. When I'm sixty-three, I don't expect that will be my number-one skill. My goal is to find a young, personable, and extroverted pastor who can build a strong youth program."

"Let me go back to a point you made earlier," recalled someone else. "You told us we have a good building at an excellent location. You're right, but you overlooked one other factor. We relocated to this site nine years ago, and I'm glad we did. It was a wise move. We completed construction of our second unit three years ago, and we're still carrying a $225,000 mortgage. I think our top priority

is to find a minister who also is an excellent administra-
tor. Our mortgage payments average nearly $600 a week!
Our top priority is meeting those payments."

"This may not sound very religious," added a fifth
member of the committee, "but we do need to be realistic.
We need a stronger financial base if we're going to be able
to meet our mortgage payments. It is three months since
our minister retired, and our offerings are running about
12 percent below a year ago. The only reason we're in the
black financially today is that we don't have to pay a full-
time minister. What we need is a pastor who can hit the
ground running and win back the loyalty and support of
those members who've moved out to the fringe or
dropped out completely. When we built this second unit,
we projected our attendance would be running close to
two hundred now, but for the past three months, it's been
averaging slightly under 120. When the people aren't
here, the money doesn't come in."

"I guess I'm the newest member of the church on this
committee," observed a man in his early fifties. "When we
moved here four years ago, we visited five or six different
churches. We finally chose this one because we liked the
intimacy and the friendliness of the people. We also
appreciated the pastor's intellectual approach to the faith.
One of the churches we visited runs close to a thousand
in three services. Another told us they average about five
hundred, and a third bragged their goal is to double in size
in five years. If we had wanted to be part of a big church,
we would have joined one of those. I agree with Chris
that we're about the right size for a family-centered
church in a world of big institutions. I think if we can
find a minister who can help us get our attendance back
up to 150 or so, we'll be able to meet all our financial

obligations and still retain the friendliness, the spontaneity, and the intimacy that so many of us cherish. If we were to double in size, as you suggest, that would require us to go to two services on Sunday morning, and I don't think you'll find much support for that in this congregation!"

"I would like to see us reach more younger families," added the seventh member of the committee. "Maybe we should look for a younger minister who can attract a younger generation. Five of the seven of us on this committee are past fifty. That suggests we're an aging congregation. There's a difference, however, between attracting more younger people and doubling in size. I would like to see us average about 150 to 160 in church on Sunday morning, but with more younger people. I think the priority should be on growing younger, not simply on getting bigger."

● ● ● ● ●

These comments illustrate at least a dozen common facets of contemporary congregational life.

1. An increasing number of denominational officials and staff members now give a high priority to numerical growth.

2. Numerical growth is not the top priority of every volunteer leader in every congregation.

3. A substantial number of lay leaders place top priority on paying all the bills on time.

4. Many volunteer leaders place a higher priority on the care of today's members than on numerical growth.

5. Parents of teenagers often place ministries with youth at the top of their list of priorities.

6. It is not uncommon for worship attendance to drop during the vacancy period between pastorates.

7. The larger the mortgage, in proportion to the size of the congregation, the more likely it will influence policy making.

8. The dream that young ministers will attract young families is still alive and flourishing.

9. Relocation of the meeting place does not automatically mean rapid numerical growth.

10. The possibility of rapid numerical growth often causes some people to be comfortable with a modest decline in numbers. For many of them, the goal is not long-term growth, but simply getting back up on that comfortable plateau.

11. For many of the people who must cope with big institutions (public schools, hospitals, places of employment, supermarkets, medical clinics, universities, shopping malls, amusement parks, etc.), the relatively small church is an attractive and comfortable stability zone.[1]

12. Many of the congregations that average 140 to 160 at Sunday morning worship find that to be an exceptionally comfortable plateau.

Six (2, 4, 9, 10, 11, and 12) of these generalizations are especially significant for those interested in encouraging congregations to move up off a plateau in size. Before looking at those issues in more detail, however, it may be useful to identify ten of the most common plateaus.[2]

Ten Plateaus

The most common plateau in size is the small church that averages 25 to 40 at worship. Typically these are tough, lay-owned, and lay-operated institutions. They are single-cell congregations that rarely reach beyond three groups of people: (1) those who are born into it, (2) those who marry into it, and (3) those rare individuals who come in on their own initiative and who are able to earn acceptance into that tightly knit fellowship. One example of the attractiveness of this size can be found in The United Methodist Church. In 1989 a total of 949 United Methodist congregations reported an average attendance at worship of between 400 and 3,374. Another 949 United Methodist congregations reported their worship attendance averaged exactly 30, while 2,943 reported an average worship attendance of between 20 and 25. A second example is the Presbyterian Church (USA), which includes six congregations with fewer than 50 members for every church with more than 1,000 members. One-fourth of all congregations affiliated with the United Church of Christ average fewer than 45 at worship.

The second most comfortable plateau is the congregation averaging 85 to 100 at worship. If it were not for the fact that the total compensation of full-time seminary trained pastors is rising faster than the rate of increase in discretionary personal income, this would be the most comfortable plateau in this whole array.

Less common, but most comfortable, is the congregation averaging 135 to 165 at worship that often can be a completely self-sufficient, autonomous, and vital church that does not feel the need for any help from outsiders.

The most uncomfortable plateau is the congregation averaging 175 to 240 at worship. Typically, this is too large to be served adequately by one minister (new missions under eight years of age do not reflect this syndrome), but too small to be able to afford, attract, and keep a competent second minister.[3]

A relatively comfortable plateau has been the multiple

staff church averaging 300 to 450 at worship. Each year, however, this becomes a less comfortable plateau as the competition from the big seven-day-a-week churches attracts a larger proportion of the generations born after 1955.[4]

While it is a more complex institution than many of the people born before 1940 find to be comfortable, the full-service church with a staff-centered ministry, averaging 500 to 700 at worship, is highly attractive to younger generations.

The seventh plateau includes a far smaller number of churches that have peaked at approximately 1,200 at worship. For them to grow beyond that plateau usually requires a radical redefinition of role, responsibilities, and relationships of the senior pastor, the staff, and the volunteer leaders. That is both difficult and rare.

A growing number of congregations find that they plateau in size at approximately 1,800 at worship. Once again an acceptance and a mastery of complexity with a larger role for volunteers in ministry often is the key to moving up off that plateau.

The next plateau, which is reached by a small number of megachurches, is approximately 2,800 at worship.

The most speculative of these is when a congregation approaches an average worship attendance of 4,500. The limitations of real estate often constitute the critical barrier for these huge churches. If they want to move beyond 4,500 at worship, that often requires an expensive capital improvements program. (A few scholars insist that an average attendance of 10,000 at worship represents an eleventh plateau, but that is not an urgent contemporary issue for most churches in North America.[5])

What Does the Majority Prefer?

Somewhere between 65 and 85 percent of all Protestant congregations founded more than a decade ago are either shrinking in number or on a plateau in size.[6] A more startling generalization is that the majority of members in the vast majority of Protestant churches on the North American continent are more comfortable with stability or decline than with the changes required to move up off a plateau in size. The status quo has more appeal than growth. Numerical growth simply is not a high priority in most churches! Taking care of today's members is a higher priority than reaching people beyond that fellowship.

Less effort is required to adjust to the changes that accompany a gradual shrinkage in size than it is to define and implement the goals required to move up off that plateau. One of the most widespread examples is the support for cutting back from two worship services to only one. By contrast, it is far more difficult to mobilize the support necessary to change from one to two worship services on Sunday morning—and especially for a proposal to offer two different worship experiences with two different choirs and two different sermons designed for two different audiences.

The comfortable plateau has broader appeal than change.

How and Why?

If the reader accepts these generalizations, two questions surface. How can a congregation move up off a plateau in size? That is the subject of the remaining chapters in this book. The more difficult question to answer is why. Why should people in a church on a plateau favor change over the status quo? Three types of responses can be offered to this second question.

The Rational Response

One response begins with the Great Commission (Matt. 28:19-20) and moves on to add that evangelism is a central teaching of the Christian faith. By definition, a Christian congregation must seek to bring others to accept Jesus Christ as Lord and Savior.

This rational explanation can be reinforced by adding: (1) an influx of new converts is the most effective single means of enhancing the vitality of a worshiping community; (2) new people help to keep the focus on meeting the religious needs of people in contrast to churches on a plateau where the emphasis often is on responding to the personal and social needs of people; (3) the numerically growing congregation is more likely to be able to retain the allegiance of the adult children of members than is the shrinking church; (4) new members can expand the sources for volunteers; (5) in today's world the choice for most North American churches is between growing older and smaller versus growing younger and larger; (6) the numerically growing organization usually provides a more supportive environment for creativity, risk-taking, and a strong future-orientation than does the numerically shrinking organization; (7) numerical growth often can facilitate a sensitive and meaningful response to the spiritual needs of that growing number of adults who identify themselves as being on a serious religious pilgrimage; (8) numerically growing congregations are more likely than churches on a plateau in size to be able to attract (a) adults born after 1955, (b) venturesome and risk-taking leaders, and (c) people with a high level of personal religious commitment; and (9) the lowest cost strategy to reverse the numerical decline of any denomination is not to plant a large number of new churches but rather to encourage at least one-half of the congregations on a plateau in size to move up off that plateau.

These rational responses to that question of why seek to move up off a plateau in size share two characteristics. First, they reflect contemporary reality. Second, they rarely are influential in persuading people in the church on a plateau to favor the changes necessary to move up off that plateau. These rational reasons are most useful in reinforcing the belief system of those already committed to change, not in winning new allies.

The Democratic Response

A remarkably popular response to this issue is to ask the people to vote their preferences. The naive approach is to state the issue in clear and simple terms. "Do you favor remaining on a plateau in size or numerical growth?" This ballot includes a choice between "Plateau" and "Growth."

The most common response evokes three patterns of behavior: (1) an overwhelming majority of the people vote for "Growth," (2) nothing happens, and (3) the absence of numerical growth eventually nurtures criticism, hostility, and internal conflict.

To state it more bluntly, by their words and votes, people may suggest they favor growth, but by their actions they usually endorse the status quo.

A better choice, if it is deemed necessary to put the question to a vote, would be to define the strategy for growth, list the resources required to implement that strategy (more volunteer teachers, creation of a second choir, additional volunteer workers, schedule changes, a high level of giving, additions to the total program, and a redefinition of staff needs), and allow people to vote by signing up to provide those additional resources.

The best that can be said for voting on the "why" question is that this is a means of publicly endorsing a strategy that already has been defined. Too often, however, that vote creates an illusion of support that does not exist. The worst that can happen is that the status quo is reaffirmed and the proponents of change are defeated and disillusioned, and a few may drop out in dismay.

The Minority Response

The most productive response to that call for a vote on numerical growth versus remaining on a plateau in size is to ignore it, to recognize that only rarely are constructive changes initiated by a majority vote, to rally that small number of people who can conceptualize a vision of a new tomorrow, to build a support group for that vision, and to provide the transformational leadership necessary to turn that vision into reality.

The most common price tag on this response is that at least a few of the people with a strong attachment to the status quo may depart. A second price tag is that the new reality rarely turns out to be an exact replica of that original inspiring vision. A third price tag is that the leaders will be well advised to err on the side of excess in communicating the vision, the goals, the required resources, and the time needed to implement that dream as they design and explain the strategy. Everything takes more time and costs more money than originally anticipated!

Why Not?

The comments and wishes articulated by the members of the call committee in the opening paragraphs of this chapter reflect a variety of hopes, but they have a common theme. All seven express a desire for a new pastor who will be, to use James Macgregor Burns's terminology, a transactional leader.[7] They hope for a pastor who can function as a combination shepherd-youth minister-administrator-fund raiser-preacher and also be able to relate effectively to younger families. In return for these services, the transaction would be balanced by providing the new pastor with economic compensation, encouragement, a cadre of volunteer leaders, and a place to do ministry. That formula calls for the transactional leader who both gives and receives in what is presumed to be an equitable and balanced exchange.

By contrast, the denominational staff person came to that Tuesday evening meeting with a radically different set of expectations based on a completely different value system and the hope that this parish would seek, welcome, and support a transformational leader.

The seven volunteer leaders came that evening with a value system that placed a premium on stability, continuity, care of those loyal aging members, an attractive ministry to teenagers, paying the bills, offsetting the shrinking numbers with younger newcomers, sound fiscal-administration, a one-to-one style of pastoral care, and re-winning the loyalty of some members who had dropped out of that parade. Those values provided the base for projecting expectations of the next minister that most likely would be satisfied by a transactional leader.

The denominational staff person walked into that meeting with a set of values that affirmed numerical growth, that placed a premium on ministries beyond today's members, that recognized the value of an attractive building at an excellent location, and that clearly endorsed the merits of the very large church. That set of values led to the articulation of a different set of expectations. It should be noted here that a clash in values is not unusual among committed Christians. That clash in values is the number-one source of conflict in the churches. It is the number-one reason for disagreements over priorities and goals. That clash in values helps to explain why the majority of Protestant churches in North America that are on a plateau in size find it more comfortable and less disruptive to watch their congregation gradually shrink in numbers rather than to implement an action plan designed to move that church up off the plateau at the cost of undermining the status quo.

The value system carried by that denominational staff person led to the suggestion that this congregation could double or even triple in size during the next dozen years. While not stated directly, this denominational staffer hoped this congregation would seek a transformational leader, not a transactional leader, as the next pastor. Such a choice could mean that this congregation, which had been on a comfortable plateau in size for many years, could be transformed into a large and numerically growing seven-day-a-week program church.

If the potential is present for that to happen, why does it not happen more often? One reason, as pointed out earlier, is that most of us are more comfortable with continuity than with discontinuity. A second reason is that most of the denominational systems for the enlistment, training, placement, and apprenticing of future pastors are designed to encourage and affirm the transactional style of ministerial leadership. This is one reason why a disproportionately large number of today's large and rapidly growing American Protestant churches either do not carry a denominational label or carry it very lightly. The independent or nondenominational congregation often offers a more supportive institutional environment for transformational leadership.

A third factor behind the contemporary shortage of transformational pastors can be found in the reward system of most congregations. That system normally will provide substantial affirmation, support, and gratitude for the energetic and productive pastor who excels in one-to-one relationships; who listens closely to everyone's problems; who becomes a reliable symbol of stability, continuity, predictability, and comfort; who genuinely loves the people; and who is reasonably effective in responding to the spiritual and religious needs of people. This reward system is most likely to be found in (a) smaller churches,[8] (b) congregations on a plateau in size, and (c) parishes that are experiencing a gradual, but far from alarming, shrinkage in numbers. These three categories include at least eight out of ten Protestant churches in North America founded before 1970.

By contrast, the congregational reward system for transformational leadership may be diluted by cries such as these: "Who gave the pastor authority to do that?" "There have been so many changes here so fast, I can't keep up with what's going on around here." "I don't see why we have to try to respond to every whim that anyone expresses." "I'm glad to see our church is growing, but I'm afraid our expenses are going up faster than our income." "I liked the old schedule where we could see everyone either before or after the one service." "I'm afraid we're spending so much effort trying to reach new people that we're neglecting our own members." "If you ask me, I thought our church was just fine the way it was when Reverend Harrison was our pastor." "Instead of asking us to become a big church, why doesn't the denomination plant more new congregations?" The transformational leader normally receives considerable affirmation, support, and enthusiastic approval from that minority of members who are deeply involved allies, but that often is diluted by clashes with the more or less silent majority over values, priorities, goals, and the power of tradition.

This combination of the attractiveness of the status quo, the influence of the institutional environment, and the power of the congregational reward system can create a self-perpetuating climate that tempts the transformational leader to take the easy way and settle into the role of the transactional pastor.

A fourth part of the explanation for why so many churches on a plateau refuse to fulfill their potential in ministry and outreach reflects the ancient question of whether the glass is half full or half empty. If the population of the community is increasing, numerical growth will be difficult because of the high level of competition among churches for new members. If the number of residents has remained approximately the same for decades, growth will be difficult because everyone who is interested in going to church already has found a church home. If the population of the community is diminishing in numbers and/or changing in terms of race, nationality, or language, growth obviously is impossible because of the absence of "our kind of people." This list of excuses is endless, but it does illustrate why expectations have such a powerful impact on performance.

Finally, in many congregations in which a dozen or more sincere, committed, and loyal members agree their church has the potential to move up off that plateau in size, nothing happens. Why? Sometimes it is that clash over values. In other churches, it may be the absence of visionary, initiating, and effective leadership. In many, however, no one is sure about where or how to begin. The purpose of this book is to suggest 44 beginning points. None fit every church. At least three or four, and maybe as many as a half dozen, will appeal to you as appropriate for your congregation. For one group of middle-sized congregations, the best beginning point may be to act their size.

CHAPTER TWO

ACT YOUR SIZE!

Why do so many congregations plateau in size with an average attendance somewhere between 25 and 240 at worship? One answer is that many are seeking to perpetuate yesterday, and yesterday has limited appeal to the generations born after 1955.

A more widespread answer is a weak self-image. The vast majority of Protestant churches on the North American continent see themselves as smaller, weaker, and with fewer resources than is true. One reason is that many once were larger and stronger and that local comparison with the past makes them appear to be small today.

A less common reason is that the reward system in a few denominations is designed to provide financial advantages to small and financially weak churches and/or those with a low level of stewardship. This may be in the form of minimal requests for the financial support of denominational agencies or as salary subsidies for the pastor or in below-market interest rates on construction loans or in financial grants. This system rewards congregations that proclaim their weaknesses and limitations.

The most highly visible factor is the rapid increase in the number of megachurches and their high visibility.

When compared to the relatively new congregation now averaging a thousand or more at worship, the typical Protestant congregation naturally will see itself as both small and severely limited in what it can do.[1] That plateau in size becomes both comfortable and justifiable. This limited self-image becomes an acceptable rationale for explaining "why we can't do that." That can be a remarkably persuasive way to kill any new idea.

"There is no way in the world we can do that," protested a member of the council at Bethany Church. "We're just an ordinary, middle-sized church, and what you're suggesting is way beyond our capabilities!"

All too often those words represent the immediate reaction when the minister proposes a new program or a new approach to ministry or expanding outreach. "That might be all right for the big churches, but we're not a big church." This response, which is all too common, suggests local resources are not adequate for the proposed course of action.

What this may represent is not the irrelevance of the proposal, but rather that the new idea was introduced prematurely or that the members underestimate their own resources.

A Better Beginning Point

In many cases that immediate rejection was the result of a weak self-image by congregational leaders. A better beginning point might have been to preface the proposal for expanding the ministry with the words, "In a congregation as large as we are," followed by the details of the suggested course of action.

This can be seen most clearly in congregations that in fact are comparatively large churches, but display the self-image of a small or middle-sized congregation. For example, what is the definition of a "big church"? A useful answer is all congregations that rank among the top 20 percent in size in that denomination, when size is measured by the average attendance at worship.

Table I reveals substantial differences among several denominations as to the size required to be among the top 20 percent in size. Near one end of the scale is the Lutheran Church-Missouri Synod, where a congregation has to average at least 240 at Sunday morning worship to be included among the largest 20 percent of the churches in that denomination. Toward the other end of that spectrum is the Church of the Nazarene, which is heavily oriented toward small congregations. In that denomination, an average attendance of 135 or more places a congregation among the top 20 percent in size.

For most of American Protestantism that figure is approximately 160 at worship, up from 150 in 1970. In other words, an average attendance of 160 or more is required today to be among the largest 20 percent of all Protestant congregations. Back in 1970 an average attendance of 150 would have placed a Protestant congregation among the top twenty in size. Some will contend the rise in this figure is a direct result of the church growth movement, which has both encouraged and enabled thousands of congregations that had been declining in numbers for many years to reverse that pattern. Others may point to the increasing number of young pastors graduating from evangelical seminaries as the key reason.

Table I

The Top Twenty Percent

The average attendance that qualifies a congregation to be among the largest 20 percent in that denomination.

Wisconsin Evangelical Lutheran Synod	245
The Lutheran Church-Missouri Synod	240
The Evangelical Lutheran Church in America	216
North American Baptist Conference	208
Evangelical Free Church	205
The Presbyterian Church (U.S.A)	175
Presbyterian Church in America	170
Assemblies of God	165
American Baptist Churches	148
United Church of Christ	145
Southern Baptist Convention*	142
Christian Church (Disciples of Christ)	140
Church of the Nazarene	135
United Methodist Church	130
Baptist General Conference	130
Free Methodist Church	110

*Average attendance in Sunday school, not worship attendance.

Certainly one factor has been the change in the models for new church development. In the 1950s, the common approach to church planting was to gather a couple of dozen people, schedule regular worship services, and hope to grow. This model produced literally thousands of new missions that leveled off with an average attendance of 65 to 125.

Today it is far more common for that mission developer team to spend several months in the field before scheduling the first worship service. A typical goal is that the first service will attract at least 250 to 300 peo-

ple and that during the critical first year, worship attendance will average at least 175 to 200. Instead of simply
starting new churches, a more widely followed model
today is an intentional effort to organize big new congregations.

This, of course, also has undercut the self-image of
thousands of long-established congregations. "I understand that new two-year-old church on the north side
averages over 300 at worship. We've been in this community for nearly a hundred years now, and for years
our attendance has fluctuated between 140 and 160.
What's wrong with us? What are they doing that we
can't do?"

For smaller congregations the statistical beginning
point may be to divide the ecclesiastical world into two
categories. The "big churches" are those in the top half
in average attendance. The small churches are those
below the median in average attendance. (The median is
the number that divides the group in half. Thus the
median age of the American population in 1990 was 32.9
years, up from 28.0 in 1970 and 30.0 in 1980. That
means that in April 1990 one-half of all Americans were
nearly 33 years of age or older and one-half were
younger.)

The median size of the congregations in a dozen
Protestant denominations, as measured by the average
worship attendance, is shown in Table II. This table
reveals that the United Methodist congregation averaging only 60 at worship and the American Baptist
church averaging 85 at worship both rank in the larger
half of all congregations in their respective denominations.

Table II

The Median Size

(as measured by worship attendance)

Evangelical Free Church	113
Evangelical Lutheran Church in America	112
The Lutheran Church-Missouri Synod	112
Wisconsin Evangelical Lutheran Synod	109
Baptist General Conference	97
Presbyterian Church in America	88
United Church of Christ	86
Missionary Church	85
American Baptist Churches	82
The Presbyterian Church (U.S.A.)	80
Christian Church (Disciples of Christ)	79
Southern Baptist Convention	75
Church of the Nazarene	72
Assemblies of God	66
United Methodist Church	56
Free Methodist Church	55

If "small" is defined as "below average," and if "average" is defined as the median, then thousands of self-identified "small churches" really are above average in size for that particular denomination.

For those who use membership as the yardstick for identifying the median, one-half of all Presbyterian Church (U.S.A.) congregations report fewer than 135 members.

What Does This Mean?

What are the implications of this weak self-image for the congregation that has been on a plateau in size for many years?

The best antidote for this weak self-image, for congregations that in fact do rank in the top half in size, is for congregational leaders to recognize that their parish is not a small church and to act their size. When compared to the vast majority of churches in their denomination, this congregation is not a little church with few resources and limited potential. All too often congregational leaders are intimidated by the very high visibility of that tiny proportion of huge churches that average 500 or more at worship.

The second implication concerns program planning. If your congregation ranks among the largest 20 percent in size in your denomination, you probably should consider offering people a choice of two different worship experiences on Sunday morning. You should think about whom you will try to reach through that new adult Sunday school class or that new circle in the women's organization you hope to organize during the next twelve months. Your ministry of music should include at least two or three choirs or instrumental groups. You probably should be thinking of a closely graded Sunday school and of a youth group for the junior highs that is separate from the senior high group. In other words, act your size as you plan the program and schedule for next year.

A third implication, and the one that will concern many leaders, is finances. The broad generalization to remember is that as size goes up, expenditures go up even more rapidly. Too often the leaders are reluctant to challenge the members with the simple fact that "acting our size" in order to move up off that plateau will require more money. While exceptions exist, the basic generalization is that congregations on a plateau in size often limit their potential by tolerating a low level of stewardship.

Frequently the initial response to the proposed budget for the coming year is "That's too much for a church as small as this one!" At this point someone might point out, "This is not a small church. Let's act our size and recognize a lot of money is required in a church as big as ours." A better response might be to refer to Jesus' admonition that to whom much has been given, from them much will be expected (Luke 12:48).

A fourth widespread implication of a weak congregational self-image often is reflected in staffing. Instead of staffing for growth, the leaders are content to staff for maintenance. As a general rule the congregation averaging 160 to 175 at worship should be served by a full-time pastor, should have a full-time church secretary, and should be in the process of adding a second person, perhaps on a part-time basis, to the program staff if the leaders expect that congregation to grow in size and to be able to assimilate new members into the life of that fellowship.

A fifth implication grows out of another basic generalization concerning church finances. The larger the size of the congregation, the larger the proportion of total member giving that will be allocated to benevolences. After deducting the money contributed to help meet the costs of staffing the regional and national agencies of that denomination, a good many small congregations contribute only 5 percent of their total member giving to missions! Middle-sized churches typically give 10 percent to missions, and large churches usually allocate 10 to 25 percent to missions. (If the cost of staffing the regional and national agencies of that denomination is defined as "missions," the combined giving for all Protestant churches of all sizes is equivalent to approximately 16 percent of total expenditures.) One expression of "acting our size" among larger churches is to increase the proportion of total expenditures allocated to missions.

Thus when the subject of giving to missions comes up, the leaders in these larger churches should be comfortable pointing out, "Since we rank among the top 20 percent in size, our mission giving should be well above the average for all churches in our denomination."

What is the best beginning point for your congregation as you seek to move up off the plateau? Could it be to act your size?

CHAPTER THREE

READ THE WARNING SIGNS!

For one large group of congregations, the beginning point in any strategy to move up off a plateau in size is to act your size, to identify, affirm, strengthen, and reinforce assets and resources and to build on those strengths in designing a church-growth strategy.

For a much smaller group of congregations the best approach is preventive maintenance. How does a congregation reverse years of gradual numerical decline or move up off a plateau in size? The best response parallels the contemporary advice on cancer. Look for the warning signs and take preventive action. The warning signs for cancer of the colon, breast cancer, and several other types of malignancies have been identified and widely publicized. The best cure for cancer begins with early detection. The best response to the tendency for congregations to plateau in size begins with recognizing the early warning signals.

From the perspective of a denominational strategy, the best approach to the tendency for congregations to plateau in size is preventive maintenance. To be more precise, this means a strategy of intervention. When the warning flags begin to appear, signaling a congregation is about to drift from a growth mode onto a plateau in size, denominational leaders should intervene to suggest corrective actions. For most denominations, however, the polity largely nullifies this option. It is a realistic alternative only for Episcopalians, Methodists, Presbyterians, and, perhaps, the new Evangelical Lutheran Church in America. Even in these highly connectional religious traditions, however, some resistance exists to this concept of outside intervention. It is extremely difficult to teach an adult something that adult does not want to learn. Likewise, it is difficult for anyone to intervene effectively in congregational life unless there is an openness, ideally an eagerness, to that intervention.

Thus in the real world the primary responsibility for recognizing and responding to these early warning signals rests on the congregational leaders.

What Are the Signals?

What are the indicators that suggest the numerically growing congregation is about to drift off onto a plateau in size or begin to experience a decline in numbers? It would be easy to offer a book-length response to that question,[1] but for illustrative purposes, this list is limited to two dozen.

1. Taking better care of today's members moves ahead of evangelism and outreach to the unchurched on the local list of priorities. The opening pages of the first chapter illustrate several expressions of this natural and predictable tendency.

2. The pastor spends more time thinking and talking about retirement a few years hence than is devoted to outreach and evangelism. A parallel signal often begins to flash when the number-one issue on the current agenda is the resolution of conflict between two staff members or between the pastor and volunteer leaders. All are diversions from ministry.

3. The average attendance at worship, which has been showing an increase year after year, begins to drop when

compared to the same months a year earlier. This often reflects a decline in the commitment level of the members.

4. The average attendance in Sunday school begins to decline. In several traditions, and especially in the South, this may be the most sensitive single indicator. In literally thousands of congregations, that first decline in Sunday school attendance was followed a few years later by the first drop in worship attendance. This also may signal a drop in the commitment level of the people.

5. The unhappy or involuntary termination of two consecutive pastorates often is followed by a plateau or decline in numbers. A parallel signal is a succession of two- to four-year pastorates.

6. One of the most subtle is in the financial contributions by members. In nearly all rapidly growing churches, the rate of increase in dollar receipts trails slightly behind the rate of increase in worship attendance. The key signal is not when the rate of increase drops. The key signal often is a decrease in the number of households that underwrite most of the annual expenditures. In one example, a numerically growing congregation discovered that 225 households accounted for 80 percent of all member contributions. Five years earlier, 263 households were needed to account for 80 percent. Even though total receipts continued to climb, that decline in the number of large contributors was an early warning signal that the congregation was about to plateau in size. That may suggest a drop in the commitment level of the key supporters.

7. A decline in the number of new members received by letter of transfer or certificate from other churches may be offset by a temporary increase in the number of new members received by other initiatory rites, such as profession of faith or baptism, but it often is a signal that this

congregation no longer is as attractive as it once was to the growing number of church shoppers. The yellow caution flag goes up when the number of people joining by letter goes down.

8. While exceptions do exist, a common early warning signal is when the total compensation (salaries, housing, pensions, health insurance, Social Security, and other fringe benefits) of the paid staff exceeds 50 percent of total member contributions. When more than one-half of total member giving is allocated to staff compensation, this often means a cutback in programming funds and/or deferred maintenance on the real estate and/or limited support for benevolences.

9. Perhaps the most subjective signal is when references to the past begin to overshadow plans, dreams, and hopes for the future of this congregation. The parallel is when tradition and precedents outweigh daring, vision, innovation, and creativity in decision making and program planning.

10. A decrease in the number of baptisms often is a signal of future numerical decline.

11. When the new minister spends more time with individuals than with groups of people, this often is an early warning sign of eventual numerical decline. A shrinking of the group life can be a highly effective means of thwarting growth.

12. A decline in the net worth of all capital assets (land, building, cash reverses, investments), after full adjustments for inflation and depreciation, often is a signal that the people are ready to rest on a comfortable plateau in size. One of the best signs of a positive future orientation, of a venturesome congregational spirit, and of an optimistic attitude is an increase in net worth.

13. If at least one-half of today's members joined more than ten years earlier, this often is a sign that the congregation has lost its capability to identify, reach, interest, attract, and assimilate new members. Likewise, if more than one-half of today's policy makers have been members for more than a decade, that often signals either a numerical decline or a plateauing in size.

14. If, week after week, nearly everyone has disappeared within ten to twelve minutes after the benediction at the close of the last Sunday morning worship service, this may be a sign of the erosion of kinship and friendship ties. The erosion of those ties often precedes numerical decline.

15. Cutting back on special worship services (Thanksgiving, Christmas Eve, Holy Week, special anniversaries, etc.) frequently is a prelude to a shift from numerical growth to a plateau or decline. Any reductions in the choices offered people often leads to numerical decline.

16. A drop in the total dollars given for missions and benevolences often parallels that shift from growth to plateau to decline.

17. An inability to design and implement a five-year plan for ministry, program, and outreach often leads to a shift from numerical growth to decline.

18. A decrease in the proportion of teenagers from outside the membership who are regularly involved in youth ministries often signals an attachment to yesteryear and an inability to respond to the contemporary needs of a new generation of youth.

19. Seniority, tenure, and kinship or friendship ties with members of the nominating committee often outweigh skill, wisdom, creativity, competence, experience in other congregations, or enthusiasm in choosing policy makers for the coming year.

20. The ratio of worship attendance to membership drops year after year.

21. The response to an impending financial problem is to concentrate on reducing expenditures rather than on increasing dollar receipts. An even more ominous expression of this signal is the temptation to seek a financial subsidy from the denomination or to use the principal in the endowment fund to cover operating costs.

22. The only significant increase in total receipts year after year is in rentals received for use of the real estate or in the size of the denominational subsidy or in income from the endowment fund.

23. While thousands of churches in retirement states such as Florida, Rhode Island, Arkansas, Missouri, Iowa, Pennsylvania, and Kansas stand out as exceptions, a useful indicator in the numerically growing congregation is the median age of the members. Most North American Protestant churches in the 1990s will grow either younger and larger or older and smaller. A rise in that median age often is a sign of future numerical decline.

24. Perhaps the most useful single indicator is in the contrast between two terms, *cut back* and *expand*. The decision to cut back on program, the Sunday morning schedule, staff, finances, weekday programming, outreach, benevolences, or office hours is often an early warning signal of future decline. By contrast, the decision to expand ministry is the most effective single antidote to institutional blight and to numerical decline.

In other words, for today's numerically growing churches, the best response to the tendency to rest on a comfortable plateau in size is to watch for those early warning signs and to initiate preventive action.

CHAPTER FOUR

QUALITY, RESPONSIVENESS, AND PRODUCTIVITY

Which congregations will be the numerically growing churches of the early years of the twenty-first century? Which denominations will report the most rapid growth in membership during the next twenty years?

One standard response to both questions is new churches. When looked at as a group, the congregations created during the past quarter century report significant net growth. While some have shrunk in size, the growth of the majority more than offsets the decline of the few. Likewise, when the membership totals are combined for congregations organized more than three decades earlier, the result is net decline. The numerical shrinkage of the majority offsets the combined growth of the minority.

From a denominational perspective, one road to numerical growth is to organize more new missions. A reasonable goal is a number equal to at least 2 to 3 percent of the current number of congregations in that regional judicatory or denomination.

A second response to that question is large congregations. As a group, the Protestant churches in North America that average more than a thousand at worship report their combined statistics represent net growth year after year. By contrast, those averaging fewer than a hundred at worship report a net decline.

That leads to a third response to that question. The numerically growing churches of the twenty-first century will be drawn in disproportionately large numbers from new congregations that quickly grow to an average worship attendance of at least three or four hundred. Likewise, the numerically growing denominations will be those that (a) organize a large number of churches and (b) encourage the emergence of an increasing number of big churches.

All three of those generalizations represent the reality of recent years. They also probably will reflect the reality of the next two or three decades. And they oversimplify reality.

For this discussion, a better beginning point would start with two different questions. First, why do new churches tend to experience numerical growth while long-established congregations tend to shrink in numbers? Second, why do large churches attract a disproportionately large number of the churchgoers born after 1955? The answers to that pair of questions offer the three best, and the three most difficult, ways to move up off that plateau in size. These can be summarized in three words: *quality, responsiveness,* and *productivity.*

Why Do They Come Back?

Millions of words have been written about the merits of inviting people to your church and on how to do that. That is important. More significant, however, is to look at why first-time visitors return the following Sunday. When asked why they returned the following Sunday, most first-time visitors give a response that can be placed in one of two categories.

The younger the visitors, the more likely they will emphasize how that first experience spoke to their religious needs. As they elaborate on this theme, they usually begin with the sermon. This may be followed by favorable comments about the anthem, the pastoral prayer, the congregational singing, the Scripture lessons, and, perhaps, participation in an adult Sunday school class or a Tuesday evening Bible study group. The focus is on finding a church that excels at meeting their religious needs.

Overlapping this set of explanations is a second group of responses that can be summarized under the umbrella of high quality. Again the quality of the preaching, if that reflects reality, usually is placed at the top of this list of reasons for coming back a second and third time. This may be followed by positive comments about the quality of the music, the quality of the welcome accorded strangers, the quality of the physical facilities, the quality of the entire worship experience, the quality of the teaching ministry, and the quality of the communication directed at first-time visitors following their departure after that initial visit.

These two paragraphs introduce the two most effective ways for a congregation to move up off a plateau in size. One strategy concentrates on increasing the frequency of participation of today's members. This often is the top priority in congregations in which the ratio of worship attendance to membership has dropped below 40 percent. The two essential components of an effective strategy for accomplishing that are (a) reduce the emphasis on institutional concerns and increase the emphasis on identifying and offering meaningful responses to the religious needs of the people and (b) improve the quality of the total ministry.[1]

An alternative strategy for moving up off that plateau in size begins with an effort to identify, contact, attract, serve, welcome, and assimilate one or both of two groups of people. The easier-to-reach group consists of newcomers to the community. The more difficult group includes residents who currently do not have an active relationship with any worshiping community.

The two essential components of an effective strategy to reach either group are (a) identifying and offering meaningful responses to the religious needs of the defined audience and (b) raising the level of quality of that ministry.

Incidentally, the emphases on concentrating on religious needs of people and on offering a high quality ministry are the central ingredients of the best advice to a new pastor. These two ingredients also are central to the strategy of what once was a numerically growing congregation that now discovers it is in a far more competitive environment in its quest for new members. These two factors also should be high priorities for the congregations reading the early warning signs identified in the previous chapter.

The Third Variable

During the past four decades the subject of the differences in productivity among people has received growing attention. One system rates the most highly productive people at 6 on a scale of 1 to 6. The least productive are rated at 1. Most adults fall in the 2 to 5 range, with 3 as an average level of productivity.

One congregation located in a community that had doubled in population in a decade registered a consistent increase in worship attendance year after year for the entire decade. The senior pastor, who rated a mark of 4 or perhaps 5 on the productivity scale, left after a dozen years. The associate minister, who was a 2 or 3 on that productivity scale, also departed. The new senior pastor, who was barely a 1, and the new associate minister, who was a 1 or 2, were the successors. What happened?

The population of the community continued to increase. A third full-time staff person, who was a 1 or 2 on that productivity scale, was added to the payroll. The congregation experienced a decline of 20 percent in worship attendance during the first year of the new staff team's tenure. The volunteer leaders were asked to accept a larger share of the work load. They accepted. The number of new members dropped sharply. During the second year the average worship attendance dropped another 15 percent. Cut backs were made in the total ministry because of the increasing shortage of participants. During the third year the worship attendance dropped by another 10 percent. In the fourth year it dropped by only 5 percent. Those who felt free to leave had left. A combination of friendship and kinship ties, denominational loyalties, the absence of convenient and attractive alternatives, tradition, habit, the sense of being needed, the reluctance to desert what several ex-members had described as a sinking ship, and guilt kept most members from leaving. For many, their level of participation declined, but they retained their affiliation with that congregation. A 2 percent decline in the fifth year was followed by four years in which that congregation drifted on a plateau in size.

At the end of nine years, a younger, more energetic, creative, venturesome, enthusiastic, future-oriented, and hard-working minister, who ranked 5 on the productivity scale, replaced the senior pastor, who chose early retirement. Within a year, worship attendance had climbed by 35 percent. The associate minister moved from barely a 2 on that productivity scale to a 3, thanks to a more positive and healthier work environment. That third full-time staff person was replaced by two part-time specialists, each of whom was easily a 4 on the productivity scale. At the end of five years, new records were being set in worship attendance, Sunday school attendance, and participation in a greatly expanded weekday program.

That new senior pastor brought the slogan "The quality goes in before the invitations go out" to every group and task force responsible for creating new programs, events, worship experiences, classes, and other points of entry for newcomers.

One way to move up off the plateau in size is to replace the low productivity staff with a more productive staff. Who has the intestinal fortitude to tackle that? The answer is few volunteer leaders! It is easier to find a new church home or to relax and to drift on that low plateau.

Ideally, and this is not uncommon, the new staff will bring not only a higher level of productivity, but also a greater sensitivity to the religious needs of people, and they will undergird that with a substantial improvement in the quality of the total ministry.

In summary, the three most promising steps up off the plateau in size may be (1) to improve the quality of every facet of church life—and this often begins with better quality preaching; (2) to be more sensitive and responsive to the religious needs of people; and (3) to get at least forty or fifty minutes of productive work out of each hour of paid staff time.

The only step that challenges excellence, a focus on meaningful responses to the religious needs of people, and high levels of productivity as the most promising path up off that plateau is initiating leadership. That subject is so important it deserves a chapter by itself, but before looking at that, another barrier to growth must be recognized.

CHAPTER FIVE

ARE YOU WILLING TO PAY THE PRICE?

One of the marvels of today's world is that a person can go into the bathroom on the second floor of a house on a hill, turn the handle on a faucet, and the water comes pouring out—except perhaps when someone is watering the lawn. That is remarkable when one recalls that the pipe bringing the water to the house comes in through the basement, and everyone knows that water runs downhill, not uphill.

The reason, of course, is not that someone has canceled the laws of gravity, but rather that the water is under pressure. When the pumps that keep the water under pressure stop working, the water runs downhill.

This introduces one of the biggest barriers that keep churches from moving up off the plateau in size. Depending on one's perspective, that barrier can be described in at least three different ways.

Wish or Will?

Perhaps the most highly visible illustration of this barrier is represented by the millions of us who are at least ten pounds over our recommended weight. It is easy to wish we could lose ten or twenty or thirty pounds during the next six months. It also is easy to find the prescription that combines a new diet with regular exercise, which, if implemented, will produce the desired weight loss. The tricky words in that sentence can be found between the two commas, *if implemented.* The key is to find the will to implement that program of diet and exercise.

Mature readers can understand this conflict between wish and will more easily than younger individuals. It resembles the conflict in the sixty-nine-year-old person between body and mind. As *Chicago Tribune* columnist Charles Leroux has pointed out, the mind may decide to go camping in a tent and spend the night in a sleeping bag on what turns out to be cold, wet, rough earth.[1] The body chooses the motel. The mind suggests a five-mile hike. The body votes for a high-cholesterol lunch. The mind supports a program to call on every newcomer to the community living within five miles of our meeting place. The body votes for the pastor to do all the visitation evangelism. The mind votes to call in a professional stewardship counselor to help raise the level of giving. The body votes to reduce expenditures. The mind votes to seek a pastor who will attract new members. The body wants a pastor who will call on today's members in their homes. The mind wants to expand the adult Sunday school program. The body opposes "giving up our room and moving to a smaller room."

Moving up off that plateau in size requires that will and the mind replace wishes and the body in the decision-making process. That is asking a lot of the sixty-nine-year-old adult—and also of the congregation resting on a comfortable plateau in size.

Subsequent chapters in this book describe a broad range of tested and proven ways for churches to move up off that plateau in size. None are worth the time required to read about them unless the will to implement a particular strategy can be mobilized. Wishing is not sufficient.

Change Versus the Status Quo

A second way to describe that barrier is to recognize that for most of us the status quo is more attractive than change. Implementing a weight-loss program requires a change in diet and/or exercise. The mind votes for the exercise. The body votes for watching football on television.

To state it in even more repulsive terms, the reason most congregations remain on a plateau in size or shrink in numbers is because their system for attracting new people is not working. It needs to be changed. Are we willing to make those changes? Usually the answer is no. It matters little whether the appropriate change is in the Sunday morning schedule or in an expansion of the financial base or in the preaching or in the Sunday school or in the meeting place or in the priorities for the allocation of the time and energy of volunteers or in the quality of the ministry or in the weekday program or in replacing a staff member or in the choice of music. The most attractive response is "Let's keep on doing what we're comfortable doing, even if it is not working." The status quo is more attractive than change.

The Three Temptations

A more sophisticated description of that barrier to moving up off the plateau in size is to picture it as three temptations.

The first temptation is close to a universal characteristic of sinful human beings. The capacity for self-delusion is without limit. An annual example of that is the thousands of high school seniors who believe their future is in becoming a professional basketball, baseball, or football player. Currently 1.3 million boys graduate from high school each year. Approximately 400 of each year's class will spend two or more years on the roster of a major league baseball, football, or basketball squad. That is one chance in 3,000 for each graduating senior boy.

Similarly, congregational leaders find it easy to persuade themselves, "This is really a friendly church" or "We don't have a parking problem" or "We have a great Sunday school" or "Perhaps I shouldn't brag, but this is the best church in town." The best test of that assumption is to count the number of church shoppers who come at least once and subsequently choose a different congregation for their new church home.

A more subtle temptation is reflected in the fact that most church members find it more comfortable and less disruptive when their congregation stops growing and begins to drift along on a plateau in size. Most adults are more at ease when surrounded by familiar faces rather than by strangers. The longtime members are pleased when tradition replaces innovation. Life becomes more predictable when that flood of strangers coming in drops off to a trickle. The theme song of the television program "Cheers" summarizes the comfort, assurance, and continuity of the familiar. Everybody knows one another correctly by name, the folks are glad we came, and we share the same troubles. The reassurance of the familiar reinforces the temptation to remain on that comfortable plateau.

The third temptation is frequently expressed in the wish for this congregation to reach large numbers of younger adults, but not change. It is tempting to hope that the style of congregational life, the sermons, the music, and the approach to corporate worship that meets the personal and religious needs of people born before 1930 will attract the generations born after 1955.

It is tempting to seek a strategy for church growth that will not require change. That misses a critical issue. The top priority in the congregation seeking to move up off the plateau is not a strategy for church growth. The real need is a strategy for planned change initiated from within an organization, plus the will and skill required to implement that strategy.

Human beings have known for centuries how to make water run uphill. The secret is for the mind to decide to pump it uphill. The problem is that when the body decides to stop pumping, the water begins to run back downhill.

Likewise, we know how to enable congregations to move up off that plateau in size. The critical issue is the will to try it and the skill to make it happen. When the will and the skill disappear, the numbers will begin to decline once again.

Since planned change is never initiated from within an organization unless (1) either discontent with the status quo is present and/or widespread perception of a crisis exists and (2) there is a willingness to pay the price of change, moving up off that plateau requires an affirmation of change. That is easier to describe than to achieve.

The Big Tradeoff

One difficulty in mobilizing the will to change is that it almost always requires a tradeoff. The heart of this tradeoff is that the effort to reach and serve new people will replace taking care of today's members as the number-one priority in the allocation of scarce resources.

"Why can't we do both?" becomes the most frequently expressed objection to that tradeoff. One explanation is that the resources to do both rarely are available. A more subtle explanation is that there is room for only one priority at the top of the current action agenda. In many churches the option of "both" is not available because they are contradictory goals. How can we change the nature of the Sunday morning worship experience and still keep it the same? How can we expand the total ministry without increasing the level of complexity? How can we bring in new people without increasing the size of the crowd?

In other words, the price of moving up off that plateau in size usually requires a willingness to pay the price of change.[2] It means a change from doing yesterday over again only better, to an intentional venture into new territory. The goalless drifting that is a characteristic of too many congregations on a comfortable plateau in size must be replaced by vision, intentionality, a venturesome spirit, and the will to pioneer new approaches to ministry. Rarely does this "just happen." Usually it is the product of visionary and initiating leadership.

CHAPTER SIX

VISIONARY INITIATING
LEADERSHIP MAY BE THE KEY

D uring the past dozen years the board of education has opened three new elementary schools plus one new junior high school, and they're now talking about a second high school that would be built on the south side," reflected a widely respected leader in a forty-year-old suburban congregation that had been on a plateau in size for more than a decade. "With that many younger families moving out here, it seems like our church should be growing, but it isn't. What should we be doing that we aren't doing to attract more people?" This comment illustrates one of the critical differences between a Protestant church and a public school system. The public schools must respond to the influx of families with young children. The church, as a voluntary association, can and often does focus on caring for the present members and can largely ignore all newcomers. By state law, children must be enrolled in school or in a home-study program. No law requires their parents to seek out a church home.

The absence of numerical growth in long-established churches located in communities that are experiencing a large influx of newcomers strikes some observers as unlikely. They assume the rising tide will lift all the ships in the harbor. One part of the explanation for what appears to be a contradiction is that the faster the rate of population growth, the larger the number of new missions that are launched, the greater the pressure on existing churches to improve and/or expand their program and facilities, and the stiffer the competition for new members. "High potential for growth" often translates into high competition among the churches. One result is that it is relatively easy for long-established churches in these rapidly growing communities to drift along on a plateau in size or to shrink in numbers.

If the community context is supportive of numerical growth, and if the will to change, identified in the previous chapter, is present, what else is needed? The answer consists of three words: *visionary initiating leadership*. All three words are important. First, someone must have a vision of what God is calling the congregation to be and to do in the years ahead. Second, that vision has to be translated into a strategy that can be implemented. Third, leadership is required that can enable the people to see the vision and to mobilize the resources required to implement that strategy.

Why do many congregations move down off that plateau and begin a period of numerical decline? Why do so few move up off that plateau?

Three overlapping reasons were identified in the previous chapter: (1) an unwillingness to change, (2) the attractiveness of the status quo or the absence of sufficient discontent with the status quo to motivate and support change, and (3) a reluctance to pay the price of change.

A fourth reason that affects perhaps 10 to 15 percent of all Protestant churches reflects the reality of demographic trends. More people are leaving than are moving into the community. This is most highly visible in scores of counties in the Great Plains where the number of deaths approaches or even exceeds the number of births. (For the United States as a whole, births in the early 1990s exceeded deaths by a 7 to 4 ratio.)

A fifth, and perhaps the most critical, reason is the absence of visionary initiating leadership. Without that leadership, it is easier to remain on a plateau or to gradually shrink in size.

What Are the Sources?

Depending on how one counts, five or six or seven sources account for most of the visionary leadership that has led congregations up off a plateau in size.

The most highly visible, of course, is the newly arrived pastor who brings a combination of transformational leadership skills, pastoral competence, persuasive communication abilities, productive work habits, an emphasis on excellence, contagious enthusiasm, attention to detail, and, most important of all, a positive vision of what God has in mind for this congregation.

A second source may be the relatively new volunteer leader who can articulate a vision of what could be and is able to win support for that vision. The critical point in this scenario is the ability of the recently arrived volunteer leader to win the unreserved support of both the pastor and at least two or three widely respected and influential longtime members for that vision. That is neither easy nor automatic!

A third possibility, which is far more common today than it was forty years ago, is when the pastor, who has functioned effectively as a transactional leader and has earned the respect of the parishioners, goes away and returns with two new pieces of baggage. One is a new and attractive vision of what the Lord is calling the congregation to be and to do. The second is a determination to master and practice the skills of a transformational leader.[1]

Where does that pastor pick up that new baggage? Most frequently that new vision comes out of intensive visits to self-identified "teaching churches" that have lived out the process.[2] These are transformed congregations where visitors can come and hear about the "before," see the "after," and discover what was done and how it was accomplished to bring about that transformation. One may be a long-established congregation that spent a decade or more on a plateau in size and now has doubled or tripled the worship attendance. Another may illustrate how to manage a successful relocation of the meeting place. A third may be a living example of how to change the culture of a congregation in order to reach a new and younger generation of people. A fourth may illustrate the switch from a focus on Sunday morning to seven-day-a-week programming.

The value of these experiences is to go and see a living model of what can happen, to talk with the people who made it happen, and to learn from their experiences. This enables some of those visitors to identify the discrepancy between "our church back home" and this living model of what could be. Out of this self-identified discrepancy may come the vision for a new tomorrow.

The understanding of the vast difference between functioning as a transactional leader versus the transformational style of leadership may come from reading or from a three- to seven-day workshop on leadership or from visits to teaching churches that also teach leadership skills or, more likely, from a combination of two or three of these.

A fourth source resembles the third, except it calls for a team of five to ten volunteer leaders to accompany the pastor on the trip to a teaching church. This often is reinforced by a reading group that expects all who will make the trip to meet together after every member has read one or two or three books that focus on that issue. The discussion in these meetings focuses on (1) the content of each book, (2) the application of the contents of the book to our situation, and (3) the listing of questions to be asked during the visit to the teaching church.

A fifth source occasionally surfaces in the complacent congregation on a comfortable plateau in size served by an overworked, but widely appreciated, minister who is a transactional leader. The sympathetic members insist on "getting help to reduce the burden on our overworked pastor." That new staff person comes on board, earns the unreserved support of the pastor, wins the loyalty and respect of the volunteer leaders, eventually articulates a vision of what could be, mobilizes the support necessary to turn that vision into reality, and everyone lives happily ever after—except for those who liked it better before all those strangers began to come here.

For reasons that may be obvious to some, but not accepted by everyone, this scenario is most likely to be acted out with a hardworking, pastoral, person-centered male pastor and a gregarious, enthusiastic, energetic, creative, determined, future-oriented, goal-driven, and hardworking laywoman as the new staff member.[3]

A sixth source may be a combination of two or three of these. One is when the newly arrived staff person begins by persuading key volunteer leaders to spend at least one long weekend every year at a teaching church. That new ad hoc alliance becomes the source of the visionary initiating leadership. Once in a while a denominational staff member may intervene, challenge the leaders with a vision of a new tomorrow, and encourage the key people to participate in a particular workshop. Occasionally the new pastor begins to build a coalition out of scattered individuals who share only two characteristics. They all are members and they all are discontented, but often for different reasons, with the status quo.

A seventh source may become the number-one beginning point for more and more congregations that seek to move up off that plateau. It begins with (1) discontent with the status quo, (2) two or three leaders (ideally one is the pastor) who agree that "something must be done," and (3) a decision to create an ad hoc long-range planning or futures committee.[4] The deliberations of this carefully selected committee become the foundation for creating and implementing a strategy for planned change initiated from within that parish.

The central point in this discussion is not numerical growth. It is the potential impact of transformational leadership that can design and implement a strategy for planned change that is initiated from within the congregation. That type of leadership is the closest to a guaranteed route up off the plateau in size.

Congregations that are about to seek a new pastor may find this to be the most attractive step up off that plateau.

Five Caution Signs

An experienced denominational staff member or a veteran pastor or a parish consultant can walk into almost any congregation that has been on a plateau for many years and, two hours later, offer a five-point prescription

for moving the church up off that plateau. That oversim-
plifies life. It is almost impossible to overstate the value of
competent visionary initiating pastoral leadership, but
that, too, can oversimplify life. On countless occasions a
highly competent, experienced, visionary, initiating pastor came to a congregation that appeared to need that
style of ministerial leadership. A couple of years later, that
pastor left, a defeated, disillusioned, and discouraged
human being filled with grave self-doubts. Why?

Mismatches Do Happen

One explanation is that it was a poor match. This was a
good congregation of good Christians seeking good leadership. They got it. But it was a mismatch between the
culture, values, and style of congregational life of that
parish and the value system, goals, definition of the
nature of a worshiping community, and perspective of
that particular minister. The best matches between a pastor and a parish resemble the relationship of the husband
and wife who have been happily married for several
decades. Only rarely do the best matches resemble the
relationship between an attorney and a client or a professor and a graduate student[5] or a bishop and the pastors in
that regional judicatory. The leadership skills of the pastor
are important, but even more critical is a good match
between pastor and parish.[6]

The Value of Long Tenure

A second explanation is tenure. Studies of congregations that have been transformed through a successful
relocation of the meeting place suggest that tends to be a

long-term undertaking. It is not unusual for twenty years to elapse between the time when relocation is first proposed and when the process has been completed.[7]

Similarly the transformation of a congregation that has been on a plateau in size for years into a numerically growing church that is reaching significant numbers of new people and fully assimilating them into the life and ministry of that parish should be seen as a long-term venture. From a ministerial perspective it is not unusual for significant changes to be visible by the end of eight months. From the perspective of the people in the pews, however, the changes tend not to be perceived as substantial and permanent until year three or four or five or six or seven of that pastorate.

It is relatively easy in the vast majority of congregations for an energetic and creative new minister to come in and boost the average attendance at worship by 10 to 15 percent within six to eight months.[8] It is far more difficult and time-consuming to create the conditions that lead to an annual net increase in membership of 5 to 10 percent year after year after year.

Excessive Impatience

Overlapping these two points is a third caution. Occasionally, the highly competent, energetic, enthusiastic, visionary, and transformational minister brings one other trait. That is excessive impatience.

The vision of a new tomorrow is both clear and compelling. The road to turning that vision into reality beckons. The recently arrived minister is impatient with those who want to move more slowly. Two years later, to the relief of both parties, that highly competent and excessively impatient minister moves on to greener pastures. What happened?

The clarity of that compelling vision caused the excessively impatient pastor to neglect to pay the rent. Many years ago, in a remarkably compelling analogy, James D. Glasse suggested that every pastor must first "pay the rent" to that parish. After the pastor has paid the three basic components of the rent (preaching and worship, teaching and pastoral care, organization and administration), Glasse writes, that minister is free to spend the balance of the discretionary time every week on other agendas.[9]

Paying the rent promptly and in full every week is the most effective way for a pastor to earn the right to introduce new ideas. Paying the rent is the best way to win respect and to acquire influence. Paying the rent promptly and in full every week can be the appropriate introductory role for the pastor who soon expands that transactional role into a transformational leadership style. Paying the rent promptly and in full often is an essential part of a larger strategy for mobilizing the resources, including allies, necessary for turning that vision into reality. This also becomes another argument for long pastorates.

Diverse Staff Expectations

A fourth pitfall for the visionary initiating leader can be found in too many large congregations. The generic name for this potential pitfall is inherited staff. The enthusiastic, energetic, venturesome, and visionary transformational leader replaces the recently retired senior pastor who was a transactional leader. The new senior pastor gathers a group of eager volunteer leaders who are convinced the time has finally arrived to make long overdue changes. An action plan is designed and approved by the governing board. What happens?

The long-tenured associate minister who had hoped to be called as the new senior pastor rallies a handful of supporters to help poison the grapevine. Another staff member uses the telephone to explain why "not much is happening now that Doctor Harrison has retired." A third staff member affirms the status quo and opposes all changes. A few months later the means-to-an-end issue of staffing has replaced the vision as the dominant item on the congregational agenda. Whether the new senior pastor wins or loses that battle over staffing matters little. The demand from many of the members is not for transformational leadership, but rather for a peacemaker who will pour oil on the troubled waters.

A parallel story could be told about when emergency repairs to the real estate or an unexpected financial crisis or moral charges levied against a staff member caused the vision to vanish.

The point of commonality is that means-to-an-end issues can create unpleasant detours for even the best of transformational leaders.

Religious or Social Needs?

Finally, one more yellow flag must be raised. Most of the suggestions offered in this book are based on the assumption that every church is organized primarily to offer meaningful responses to the religious needs of people. That is a misleading assumption! As the decades have rolled past, thousands of congregations on a plateau—or shrinking in numbers—have evolved so that responding to the religious needs of people has become a secondary priority. Today these churches are held together by a combination of factors that often include (1) kinship and friendship ties; (2) local traditions; (3) a powerful orientation toward and affection for yesterday; (4) inherited (not earned) denominational loyalties; (5) attachment to this sacred place filled with rich memories; (6) a shared value system; (7) a common nationality, language, racial, or ethnic heritage; (8) habit; (9) the fact that it is easier and more comfortable to worship God in the company of longtime friends in a familiar setting than in a strange place filled with strangers; and (10) affection and respect for a long-tenured and person-centered pastor who excels in care of the members.

The reason that congregation is attracting few new members who are not already related to a member is simple. Those ten factors tend to be exclusionary ties. They bind together those who are already part of the congregation into a closely knit fellowship. They also cause strangers to feel excluded. First-time visitors who come for religious reasons do not return.

For these congregations to be able to move up off that plateau in size requires a transformation in the value system. Identifying and providing meaningful responses to the religious needs of people must become the top priority. That transformation becomes the first order of business for the initiating leader. Sometimes that must begin by redefining the agenda of the governing board of that parish. That often requires the skills of the transformational leader.

CHAPTER SEVEN

SHARPEN THE FOCUS!

I f you ask me, and I realize no one has, but I've been a
member here for nearly three years now, and I am a
member of the church council, so I'm-entitled to
express my opinion," declared a young architect who had
married a third-generation member of Central Church. "I
think we ought to sell this property and build new on a
large site at a better location. The sanctuary is on the second floor; we have only two good Sunday school classrooms, both on the third floor; the nursery is a moldy
room in a corner on the first floor that is below grade; and
we own a grand total of six off-street parking spaces. If we
want to reach a new and younger generation of people,
we need better facilities."

"All of this talk about trying to attract more young
families sounds good," commented one of two fourth-
generation members on the church council, "but I think
we owe something to the people who have helped keep
this church alive all these years. I believe our first priority
should be to take better care of our older members and
shut-ins. I know a lot of them feel neglected."

"This may not be the place to talk about it, but most of
you know our most pressing problem is within the staff,"
declared the chairperson of the personnel committee at
this monthly meeting of the church council at Central
Church. The pastor had asked them to identify what they

saw as the most pressing problems. Just as the young architect was finishing his comments, the pastor left to answer the telephone. His departure opened the opportunity for the next two complaints. "Most of you know our secretary, who has been with us for nearly twenty years, feels our new minister is incompetent, rude, and lazy. He claims she is trying to be his boss. Our part-time educational assistant complains the new minister is not supporting her program. The pastor wants to replace both of them."

"That raises another issue," interrupted the chairperson of the Christian education committee as he heard the pastor coming down the corridor. "We really do need to take a look at our new schedule. The idea of running Sunday school concurrently with worship was adopted in the hopes it would attract families with young children, but I don't believe it's working. We've attracted only a couple of new families since we adopted this schedule, and they're both older couples. In addition, the new schedule has undercut our whole adult education program."

"I know this will sound like a broken record," the treasurer began in an apologetic tone of voice, "but last month was the fifth consecutive month in which our expenses exceeded our income. That has never happened before in my eleven years as church treasurer. Our reserves are down to less than $6,000, and if this pattern doesn't change, we'll soon have a crisis."

"I hate to be the bearer of bad news," commented a trustee, "but this morning a friend of mine, who is a roofing contractor, came over to inspect the roof. The trustees had expected the repairs could be made for somewhere between $3,000 and $5,000. This contractor told me the wood underneath the shingles has rotted to the point that a complete job will probably cost close to $60,000."

"Well, that's one more argument to relocate," observed the young architect.

"When my wife and I joined this church back in 1967, we reported nearly 900 members," reflected the oldest member of the church council. "For the past several years we've been reporting right around 400. I think we need a drive to enlist a bunch of new members so we can pay our bills."

• • •

While the details vary, this brief account illustrates one of the most common barriers to moving up off a plateau in size. The agenda is overloaded with means-to-an-end issues. The best location for the meeting place is a means-to-an-end issue. The resolution of the conflict among the staff is a means-to-an-end issue. The Sunday morning schedule is a means-to-an-end issue. The financial squeeze is a means-to-an-end issue and perhaps a symptom of other problems. The repair of the roof is a means-to-an-end issue. The need to attract new members to help pay the bills is at best an institutional survival issue and at worst a counterproductive approach to enlisting new members. The plea for better care of the older members and the shut-ins may be a ministry concern—or it may be another expression of congregational self-centeredness.

What Can Be Done?

If and when the leaders of this congregation decide to make the effort required to enable this aging and shrinking congregation to reverse that pattern of numerical decline, it will be necessary to change the agenda. Instead of responding to the series of unexpected crises, the church council should redefine its role. Rarely is that easy, but it is possible, and attractive choices do exist.

The first, and the most obvious, would be to delegate to committees the issues that have usurped the agenda of the church council. A special ad hoc committee could be appointed to study the related issues of the roof and the possible relocation of the meeting place. The worship and Christian education committees could be instructed to form a joint task force to review the schedule. The personnel committee could be asked to work on resolving the conflict within the staff. The finance committee could be asked to consider a special short-term financial campaign to solve the cash flow problem. The committee on congregational care could be asked to organize a group of volunteers to call regularly on shut-ins and older members. This would free the church council to concentrate on the redefinition of the role of this congregation and on specific long-term goals.

A second possibility would be to create a special ad hoc futures committee that would be charged with redefining the role of this congregation and recommending an action program.[1] That action program would be the foundation for subsequent recommendations on a permanent meeting place, the Sunday morning schedule, the staffing configuration, and a long-term financial strategy.

A third possibility could be to appoint an ad hoc study committee with a more narrowly focused two-part assignment. This committee would be asked to examine the local setting, to identify the distinctive strengths and assets of this congregation, and to recommend which slice of the total population the congregation should seek to reach and serve. The second half of the assignment would be to bring in specific recommendations on real estate, staffing, schedule, and finances that would enable this congregation to reach and serve that precisely defined audience.

A fourth alternative, which is suggested by that "one-hour package" schedule and the unprecedented financial squeeze, would be to appoint a special ad hoc study committee to examine two sides of the same basic question. First, has this church been drifting in the direction of becoming a low-commitment congregation? Second, if the evidence suggests that has been the pattern, what steps must be taken to raise the commitment level? (In today's world, the most common difference between numerically growing congregations and those on a plateau in size or declining in numbers is commitment. High commitment churches, which project high expectations of people, are far more likely to attract the generations born after 1955 than are the low commitment churches.) If the conclusion is that this has become a low-commitment church and little interest exists in changing expectations, this may mean the top priority should be on reaching people born before 1935.

While these alternatives do not exhaust the list of possibilities, they do illustrate the central point of this chapter. The congregation that wishes to move up off a plateau in size probably will have to replace the means-to-an-end issues that now dominate the agenda with a stronger focus on role, direction, ministry, outreach, goals, and the priorities that will direct the allocation of scarce resources.

Who will accept the responsibility for replacing means-to-an-end issues with long-term ministry goals at the top of the agenda? The pastor? A volunteer leader? The governing board? After that decision has been made, it may be feasible to begin to examine possible next steps.

CHAPTER EIGHT

WHAT DO WE DO NEXT?

A t this point the impatient reader may be more than ready to switch the focus from the congrega-tional context to a discussion of specific action steps. How can we move up off this plateau in size?

The three most promising steps were identified in the fourth chapter. One is to improve the quality of the total ministry. This includes everything from the teaching ministry to the nursery to the preaching to the music to parking. A second is to focus on meeting the religious needs of people. This often requires radical changes, including a lower priority for responding to the social needs of people. The third is to improve the level of productivity of the paid staff.

How Much Change?

If none of those three steps appears to be appropriate for your situation, it may be wise to begin by examining another question: How much change are you willing to support?

One Saturday afternoon in June, twenty-seven-year-old Ralph Adams and twenty-four-year-old Carol Baxter were married. Carol had just completed her third year as an elementary school teacher. Several weeks after their ten-day honeymoon, Carol returned to the classroom for her fourth year. The following March she was delighted to discover she was pregnant, so she did not return to teaching. The baby was born in November. Twenty-three months later, baby number two arrived. Three years later, a third baby was born to this happy full-time homemaker and her delighted husband. Ralph had been working for the state government for five years when they were married, and by the time the third child was born, Ralph had received two major promotions.

On that same Saturday afternoon in June, a thousand miles away, twenty-seven-year-old Jack McGuire and twenty-four-year-old Susan Welsh were married. Susan was in her third year as an editor with a large publishing house. She kept her name for personal and professional reasons. Eight years later, after two job changes, Susan was the editor-in-chief of a trade magazine. She also realized that her biological clock was running, and she was anxious to become a mother. A year later she gave birth to twins. Twenty-one months later, Susan gave birth to healthy triplets. Thanks to the combination of her widowed mother, who came to live with them, a nanny, a sympathetic publisher, a cooperative husband, and a remarkably talented administrative assistant, Susan was able to continue as the editor-in-chief of that trade magazine.

Twelve years later, on a beautiful day in June, each couple celebrated their twelfth wedding anniversary. Ralph and Carol were the proud parents of a ten-year-old son, an eight-year-old daughter, and a five-year-old daughter. They looked back over twelve wonderful years filled with a sense of continuity and incremental change. The summer after their son was born, they moved from an apartment into a single-family home where they still lived.

Ralph was enthusiastic about his current job as the number-two person in the same state department where he had begun working seventeen years earlier. This was a happy household of five people.

Jack McGuire and Susan Welch celebrated their twelfth wedding anniversary that same day. Several months after the birth of the triplets, Susan had resigned her position at the trade magazine to become a part-time consultant to other trade magazines and was able to do much of her work out of her home, but she had to make about forty overnight trips a year. Jack was satisfied with what was his seventh job since college. Their nine-person household included Susan's mother and a live-in housekeeper, plus the five unbelievably active children. As they looked back over those twelve years together, they agreed their life had been filled with discontinuity, sudden changes, surprises, and more surprises. "If someone had told me this is what the next twelve years would bring," reflected Susan, "I'm not sure I would have been so eager to marry you. But I'm glad I did."

Ralph and Carol Adams had followed a road marked by considerable continuity. Susan Welch and Jack McGuire had enjoyed twelve years together that were filled with discontinuity.

The moral of these stories for churches seeking to move up off a plateau in size is a question: Do you prefer to maximize continuity, or are you willing to experience considerable discontinuity? That question should be answered before choosing the next step.

What is the difference? One difference, of course, is how much change you are willing to experience. A second, and less obvious, difference is that continuity usually means modest numerical growth, while the price of rapid numerical growth often is discontinuity. This is illustrated by the analogy used earlier. Jack and Carol Adams went from life as a childless couple to the parents of three children in five years. Susan Welch and Jack McGuire, after nine years of living as a childless couple, in less than two years found themselves living in a nine-person household with two other adults and five children under two years of age.

Two Examples of Discontinuity

Most adults strongly favor continuity over discontinuity. This normal, natural, and predictable resistance to discontinuity is one of the most widespread barriers to moving up off a plateau in size. A common example is the long-established congregation that has been on a plateau in size as it averages between 135 and 165 at worship year after year. Several months after arriving, the new minister proposes the Sunday morning schedule be expanded as part of a church-growth strategy. Since the sanctuary was designed to seat 300, this proposal arouses considerable resistance. "We do not have a space problem, so why change to two services? All that will do will be to increase the level of anonymity by dividing us into two congregations."

The local tradition of "be kind to the new minister during that honeymoon first year" enables the new pastor to prevail. The governing board adopts (which is not the same as approving or supporting) the new schedule. The forces for continuity, however, do not surrender completely. They insist on seven conditions: (1) the services will be carbon copies except for the time of day; (2) the same bulletin will be used at both services; (3) the chancel choir will sing at both services; (4) to perpetuate the traditional summer slump, only one worship service will be scheduled for ten Sundays from mid-June through August; (5) the chancel choir will continue to be on vacation during the summer; (6) the Sunday school will continue to cut back to two classes for children, one for youth, and one for adults during that ten-Sunday summer period; and (7) none of the pews will be removed from the nave to create the feeling of a "full church" when fewer than a hundred worshipers are present.

The new minister, who has misidentified a single tactic (two services) as a strategy for church growth, agrees to all seven conditions. A year later, worship attendance averages 55 at the first service and 105 at the second, up 10 percent from the 145 during the predecessor's last year.

Two and one-half years after the new schedule becomes effective, that pastor accepts the opportunity to move to another church. Shortly before departing, he confides to a friend, "I feel I've accomplished everything I can here, and I'm leaving this congregation larger and stronger than it was when I came."

The next pastor, who is a person-centered individual with a deep need for the approval of others, arrives and sets out to call on every household in that parish as soon as possible. The proponents of continuity make it clear to this listening ear that they prefer the old schedule, which reinforced "the feeling that we are one big family here."

During that summer, an apparently spontaneous groundswell of opinion sweeps across the parish "that when September arrives, let's continue with only one service with Sunday school followed by church." The new minister openly, but not aggressively, supports this desire to recreate yesterday. With only three dissenting votes, the governing board approves (not simply adopts) a motion to return to the old schedule. A year later, the worship attendance is averaging 152. Two years later, it is 143, and everybody, except the members of the finance committee, who are worried about the cash flow problem, is happy. Continuity with the past generates a greater feeling of comfort than does discontinuity.

A far more radical example of discontinuity can be seen in one strategy used by congregations averaging between 600 and 800 at worship who seek to move up off that plateau. This strategy usually calls for five different expressions of discontinuity.

Perhaps the most crucial strategy is to shift from institutional needs and functions (Christian education, administration, worship, youth ministries, missions, music, evangelism, etc.) to staffing ministries for people. Examples of this include replacing the director of Christian education with someone who will expand the group life through the teaching ministry; replacing the youth minister with a person who will help to create and oversee a huge package of ministries with families that include teenagers; replacing the choir director(s) with a staff person(s) who understands the unique power of music as a channel for expressing one's creativity, as a communication tool that can be more powerful than language, and as an essential component of large group events; replacing the children's worker with someone who will build a network of ministries with families that include young children; replacing the senior pastor, who has functioned as a self-identified "directing minister" (which is an appropriate role in the congregation satisfied to remain on a plateau averaging 350 to 500 at worship), with a delegating pastor; replacing the minister of missions who raised money and enlisted volunteers to work in mission activities with a staff member who works with a few innovative souls to create new responses to new needs and inspires many others to accept active involvement in missions as a normal part of a Christian's response to God's love; replacing the parish visitor or minister of pastoral care with a person who enlists and trains volunteers to do pastoral care; replacing the minister of evangelism who identified, visited, and enlisted new members with someone who enlists and trains teams of evangelists; and, most difficult of all, replacing that minister who occupied the pulpit for all worship services on forty or more Sundays a year with a senior minister who pursues an annual goal of "creating one more new weekly worship experience that will be different from anything else we now do and thus will enable us to reach and respond to the religious needs of an audience we're now missing."

While a few leaders find it easy to adapt to this new role for paid professional members, most cannot. To assume an individual employed to fill one role will be happy, comfortable, and productive in a radically different role is an extravagant expectation. That old saying "If you want to change the game, begin by changing the players" is relevant to this scenario.

A second and far more common expression of a strategy of discontinuity is to replace the severely introverted, task-oriented, low energy, and comparatively inept pastor with a person-centered, extroverted, high energy, exceptionally competent, and highly productive successor who possesses a magnetic personality. That magnetic personality may replace the denominational label, local traditions, the program, the community image, the reputation, and earlier priorities as the number-one variable in why church shoppers pick that congregation as their new church home. This strategy wins far more support from the laity than it evokes from the clergy!

A third expression of that strategy of discontinuity is to help at least three-quarters of the members find their primary institutional identity with a class, study group, circle, choir, mutual support group, mission team, cell, or some other expression of volunteer ministry rather than with that congregation as a whole. Both longtime members and newcomers must look for intimacy in the group life. Only rarely will people find that desired intimacy in the congregation or in relationships with the staff.

A fourth and extremely difficult expression of the strategy filled with discontinuity is to replace the image of that church as a parcel of sacred real estate with the image of a worshiping community. (One test is that the self-identified worshiping community finds it relatively easy to relocate the meeting place while a proposal to relocate naturally will be a highly divisive issue in the real estate-centered church.)

A fifth, and perhaps the most subtle and most controversial, expression of this strategy of discontinuity for the congregation seeking to move up to a thousand or more in average attendance concerns the primary criteria for selecting and evaluating staff. This strategy calls for competence, creativity, character, energy, initiative, persistence, productivity, and performance to be given far more weight than the academic credentials, charm, age, seniority, tenure, or personality in selecting and evaluating program staff, including the ordained members of that staff.

A quick review of these five expressions of discontinu-

ity explains why the vast majority of Protestant churches
on the North American continent average fewer than
180 at worship and why so few average more than 900.

These two examples of strategies built around discontinuity are offered to illustrate why that comfortable
plateau often appears to be so attractive.

The second example also illustrates a crucial question:
How much discontinuity will your people tolerate?

The distinction between the attractiveness of continuity and the threatening nature of discontinuity also can
be illustrated by looking at potential next steps. Seven
steps, each one filled with the potential for rapid numerical growth, share the common characteristic of substantial discontinuity with the past. Many more alternatives,
each one of which can be a productive first step up off
that plateau, call for far less discontinuity. Which road do
you prefer? Perhaps the best way to make that decision is
to look at the two maps.

The Road of Discontinuity

1. Focus on Cohorts, Not Individuals

The attractive temptation in most congregations is to
wish for a larger choir, new members for the adult Sunday
school class, fresh faces to teach in the children's division,
a few younger women for the women's organization, a
couple of additional ushers, two more tenors, and more
contributors to the budget.

Undergirding that wish is the hope that we can add a
few more new members each year and ideally they will be
like us, only a little younger. It is assumed every new
member can and will fit into the existing organizational

structure. If that hope can be fulfilled, the result will combine numerical growth and continuity.

A radically different step up off that plateau is to seek to reach groups of people. One could be a new Sunday school class of newlyweds in their first marriage. A second could be a new circle in the women's organization consisting of single-parent mothers. A third could be a new choir composed of young childless couples and never-married young adults. A fourth could be a new Thursday afternoon Bible study group for empty-nest mothers. A fifth could be a new Sunday school class for middle-aged adults in their second or subsequent marriage. A sixth could be a new mutual support group for adult children of an alcoholic parent. A seventh could be a Sunday school class for parents of twins.

The focus on individuals often (a) reinforces continuity, (b) attracts replacements for departing members, and (c) may or may not result in modest numerical growth. The focus on reaching groups can produce rapid numerical growth, but the price tags usually include discontinuity, greater complexity, and increased anonymity.

2. Preach Not to the Choir, But to the Pilgrims

The general tendency for the pastor of a church on a plateau is to prepare sermons designed to enlighten the members, to strengthen their faith, to comfort them in times of despair, to affirm God's love, and perhaps occasionally to challenge the members to a stronger commitment to be disciples of Jesus Christ. If either the content or the delivery is well above average, the members will be satisfied. If both content and delivery are far above average, the members may begin to urge friends, neighbors,

colleagues at work, and relatives to attend. If both content and delivery are far above average week after week,
that minister probably will be invited to move to a larger
congregation. If both content and delivery are below
average week after week, that congregation probably will
move down off that plateau in size.

An alternative is to prepare sermons designed for adults
on a self-identified religious pilgrimage. These sermons
often are built around two story lines. One story line is an
exposition of a specific biblical passage or a doctrine of
the Christian faith or a central component of the faith.
The second story line is designed to persuade the listeners
that this is the answer to that faith question with which
they have been struggling. Some preachers reverse those
two story lines and begin with the faith question.

Most members find this to be enlightening, meaningful, and affirming. The pilgrims, searchers, seekers, and
others on a faith journey leave convinced, "I want to
come back and hear more." If both content and delivery
are well above average, this approach to preaching can
increase the frequency of attendance of the current membership and also persuade the shoppers, searchers, seekers, and pilgrims that this is the church for them. The
goal is not simply more members, but rather new converts.

3. Add a New Ministry

The closest to a guaranteed step up off that plateau in
size is to create a multi-faceted package of ministries with
families that include young children. The centerpiece of
that package is the Christian day school. This often
begins with a nursery school for three- and four-year-old

children. Two years later kindergarten is added. The following year first grade is added. The next year the school is expanded to include second grade, and third grade is added the following year. A dozen to two dozen other components constitute the entire package. These may include a Mothers' Club, a Parents' Day Out program, a new Sunday school class for parents of young children, parenting classes, a coed volleyball league, a circle in the women's organization for new mothers, a Men's Bible and Prayer Breakfast, and, in larger congregations, a coed football team.

Other possibilities include mission work camp trips to another continent, a ministry with young never-married adults and childless couples, a singles group for the formerly married, an athletic program, a seven-day-a-week ministry with mature adults, or a program to help alleviate world hunger.

The crucial issue in choosing this step is to distinguish between offering one more community service program versus creating a new ministry that is completely integrated into the worship and teaching ministries of that parish. The first calls for a landlord role. The second can produce substantial numerical growth, but the price tags include greater complexity and considerable discontinuity as well as that unwelcome increase in anonymity.

4. Relocate the Meeting Place

For thousands of congregations this has been (a) the critical first step off that plateau to rapid numerical growth, (b) disruptive discontinuity with the past, (c) the most effective means of revitalizing a complacent congregation, and (d) a twenty-year process.[1]

5. Expand the Sunday Morning Schedule

For many longtime, contented, and passive members, the most threatening step up off that plateau is represented by an expansion of the Sunday morning schedule. The proponents of the change often are surprised by this hostile response when other major changes were not challenged. The explanation often is simple. The other changes could be ignored. Some had very low visibility. Changing the Sunday morning schedule, however, produces two threats. Will it affect my personal routine? Will it mean I will not see all my friends every Sunday?

From a tactical perspective, this often means it is wise, if possible, to continue the present schedule unchanged and add to it. Frequently, however, that cannot be done. That means changes that create discontinuity.

While the Sunday morning schedule should reflect local values, goals, and unique circumstances, a useful beginning point often is two or three different worship experiences with Sunday school sandwiched between the early and late worship services.[2]

In larger congregations this may include two different worship experiences offered at the same hour. The traditional service will be in the sanctuary, while the non-traditional worship experience may be held in the parlor, the fellowship hall, or the gymnasium.

6. Build a New Staff

When a professional baseball team fails to win at least one-half of its games year after year, a common result is the dismissal of the manager. One of the most difficult assignments for that new baseball manager is to explain to an aging veteran "the time has come to hang it up. We are letting you go."

The most distasteful assignment for volunteer leaders in a congregation is to inform the pastor, "We believe we need a change in our ministerial leadership." In other congregations the decision is to replace a staff member. In at least a few, the time has come to build a new staff for a new day.

One reason may be a severe mismatch between the competencies or personality of a particular staff member and that congregation's needs. In other churches it may be the need to find a more productive staff member. For some pastors, obsolescence came before retirement. For larger congregations, this may mean replacing a transactional-style leader with a transformational pastor. One reason that is exceptionally difficult is the widespread shortage of transformational pastors. Another is the attractiveness of the status quo. A third is that for many members it would be easier to drop into inactivity or to change churches than to tackle this sensitive subject.

For many congregations that have been on a plateau in size for years, or even shrinking in numbers, this may be the logical first step. The price tag, however, is not simply discontinuity. It also may include swapping the known for the unknown, guilt, the termination of longtime friendships between supporters of the pastor and those who are convinced that the time has come for a change, stress, and, perhaps, money. (In some traditions the congregation gives the pastor a substantial sum of money for a letter of resignation or an announcement of early retirement.)

7. *From Low Commitment to High Commitment*

The most subtle of these seven steps that include a substantial degree of discontinuity with the past rarely happens except following the arrival of a new pastor.

Typically the new pastor brings a set of higher expectations and models, by personal behavior, those higher expectations. These higher expectations often include (a) a demanding quest for excellence, (b) thorough preparation before coming to a meeting, (c) weekly (or more frequent) participation in corporate worship, (d) tithing by all leaders, (e) participation by all leaders in the teaching ministry to model the importance of that ministry, (f) a greater emphasis on the power of intercessory prayer, and (g) high standards of behavior for all leaders.

Although exceptions do exist, the basic pattern in American Protestantism is that numerically growing congregations tend to project higher expectations of their members than do numerically shrinking churches. Likewise a decline in the level of expectations often is followed by a decline in the level of commitment by the members and by a decline in the number of first-time visitors who return.

Each one of these seven steps typically results in substantial discontinuity with the past. In some congregations that is an acceptable price to pay for moving up off the plateau. In others the attachment to the past, the comfort of the status quo, and the style of leadership may cause people to conclude that the price is too high.

For those who place a higher value on continuity and who prefer an incremental approach to change, several other possibilities merit consideration.

Continuity with the Past

1. Carve Out a Niche

Perhaps one of the least threatening steps up off the plateau begins with the assurance, " We'll keep on doing everything we have been doing." This is followed by identifying one slice of the local population that is not being served adequately by the other churches in the community. This may be single-parent mothers, post-high school young adults, divorced men, one-person households, families that include a developmentally handicapped member, couples in which one or both are in their second marriage, young never-married men, the hearing impaired, undergraduates at a nearby college or university, or couples in an interfaith marriage.

One parallel is the metropolitan newspaper that publishes a half-dozen different editions. One edition is directed at the largely black population residing on the south side, another to the largely Hispanic west side, a third to a high-income cluster of suburban communities to the north, a fourth to a working class, largely Anglo area on the east side, and a fifth to a middle income suburban county to the west. The sixth is the last edition, which includes the previous night's West Coast baseball scores and the latest financial news. It is sold at downtown newsstands to commuters as they come to work.

Another example is the contrast between the weekly magazine *Sports Illustrated* and the tabloid newspaper *The National Enquirer*. Both enjoy a circulation of approximately 3.5 million. The former has carved out a prosperous niche consisting largely of upscale readers interested in professional sports. It achieves that goal by direct mail advertising to a carefully selected audience. One result is that an exceptionally high percentage (nearly 96 percent in 1990) of the circulation is by subscription. *The National Enquirer* also has carved out a highly prosperous niche, but 90 percent of its 3.5 million circulation is at newsstands, including checkout aisles at supermarkets. Each of these two periodicals has a distinctive niche, but they have limited overlap and use two different channels for reaching their readers.

Similarly, two congregations carrying the same denominational label may meet in buildings only a few blocks apart. The smaller concentrates largely on reaching mature adults who enjoy being with one another, and it covers the broad middle of the theological spectrum. The larger may focus on reaching and serving the generations born after 1945 who seek a theologically more conservative approach to the faith in a high-commitment congregation.

In a larger community with four congregations from what is now one denomination, the distinctive niche may be represented by a place on the theological spectrum. One congregation may appeal to the evangelicals, another to the liberals, a third to the self-identified charismatic Christians, and a fourth to those who identify themselves as "in the middle of the theological road."

Other possibilities are the "international church" that draws people from two or three or four dozen nationalities, the tithing church, the teaching church, the racially integrated church that attracts interracial couples, or the congregation that is organized around volunteer involvement in and the financial support of world missions.

The second step requires acquiring the level of expertise appropriate for that niche. The best way is to spend three to seven days in a teaching church that is carrying out an effective ministry with that group of people. The second best is workshops. A third is books. A fourth is to add an experienced specialist on that phase of ministry to the staff.

The third step is to decide who will do it. This may be in the form of a new task force or a new Sunday school class or a new circle in the women's organization or one staff member with volunteer allies or by adding another worship service to the schedule. Ideally at least one or two widely respected and influential members will be actively involved in helping to make this new ministry happen.

The fourth step is to do it.

2. Settle Existing Quarrels and Disputes

By far the best beginning point for severely polarized or badly divided congregations is to resolve that dispute. Until that has been accomplished, it is unlikely strangers will accept this as a hospitable environment.

3. Solve the Financial Problems

When survival goals, and especially a severe financial squeeze, dominate the agenda, it may be impossible to implement any strategy for moving up off that plateau in size. For thousands of congregations, the logical first step is to resolve the financial problem. This may require raising the level of financial support from the members. It may mean reducing expenditures. Rarely is a financial subsidy from denominational headquarters the best solution. That often creates dependency, not self-sufficiency.

4. Improve the Real Estate

While this is a means-to-an-end subject, in at least a few churches the first logical step will be to improve and/or expand the meeting place. This may mean adding more off-street parking or remodeling the narthex to provide a more attractive setting for greeting people or creating better quality meeting rooms or air conditioning the most heavily used rooms or replacing the roof or constructing an addition or acquiring additional land. The decision makers must perceive this as a necessary preliminary step, not as an end in itself.

5. Expand the Number of Entry Points

This may be easier said than done, since many of the existing classes, groups, choirs, and circles will insist the top priority should be on funneling newcomers into their groups to replace those who have left.

The key word is *new.* The central dynamic is to create new groups for new people. Do not expect long-established groups to attract new members! A far more attractive alternative is to invite future members to help pioneer new groups, classes, programs, events, choirs, circles, and cells. Recognize the need to not threaten the role or place of long-established groups. Ideally this will be seen as part of the change-by-addition strategy described in alternative step 15 in this chapter.

6. Change the Style of Ministry

Perhaps the most difficult to explain of these potential next steps requires a change in the style of ministry. At least a majority of pastors and the vast majority of the laity enjoy a style of ministry built around one-to-one relationships. This offers tremendous satisfaction to many ministers and to most members. Everyone enjoys that close one-to-one relationship between the pastor and each parishioner.

The drawback is that this is a highly labor intensive approach to ministry. If the congregation is to grow in numbers, that probably means replacing the style of ministry with a different role for the pastor. This new role calls for the pastor to spend more time with groups of people and less time in one-to-one relationships.[3] That is extremely difficult for either the clergy or the laity to accept and affirm. It is easiest to accept when that new role is introduced by the newly arrived pastor. The change of pastors reduces the sense of discontinuity in the style of ministry.

7. Expand the Ministry of Music

This usually requires two changes. Normally both meet with substantial opposition. One change is to broaden the range of hymns and anthems and to supplement the piano and/or organ with a number of other musical instruments.

The second change is to increase the number and variety of musical groups, both vocal and instrumental. This often creates highly attractive new entry points for newcomers. It also is a means of appealing to a more diverse audience. It also can fuel the fire that calls for a change in pastors if this is widely perceived as a severe break in the continuity with the past. A common way to offset this is to design one worship service that features great continuity with the past in music while the discontinuity in music is limited to the other hour.

8. Enlist a New Cadre of Volunteer Policy Makers

If implemented gradually over two or three years by a system of rotation-in-office, this will be less threatening to those who place a high value on continuity.

This step often wins broad support and can be an effective channel for welcoming both new people and new ideas. It may be the most acceptable means of replacing a powerful past-orientation with a creative future-orientation. It is one of the most widely followed means of replacing survival goals with ministry goals at the top of the list of priorities. It can be a creative way to produce allies for change.

The fearsome price tag is that this means a transfer of control from longtime members to new members. Some longtime leaders may prefer to seek a new pastor rather than surrender the control they have earned (or inherited).

9. Expand the Teaching Ministry

One of the least controversial and most likely to succeed initial steps up off that plateau in size is to greatly expand the teaching ministry. This usually means adding new weekday classes as well as expanding the adult Sunday school and making learning one of the major components of the youth ministry. Each new class also represents a new entry point for future new members.

10. Change the System of Governance

One of the most difficult steps to implement is to change the self-identified role of the governing board.

Instead of concentrating its efforts on administration, finances, real estate, receiving reports from committees, overseeing the work of the pastor, and coordinating the schedule, these are all delegated to committees and task forces and/or to staff. The central purpose of the governing board is redefined to devising and implementing a strategy to move up off that plateau in size. A book like this one replaces *Robert's Rules of Order* or the denominational book of church order as the number-one reference tool for the board. Ministry replaces administration as the theme of the monthly meetings of the governing board.

In several denominations the polity prohibits such a radical step. The alternative is to create a special ad hoc committee and give it this responsibility.[4] The problem with that alternative is that ad hoc committees often do not possess the authority that the governing board has in order to implement a plan of action.

11. Strengthen the Organizational Life

An attractive alternative for the small to middle-sized congregation begins with reconceptualizing the nature of this parish. Instead of perceiving it as a congregation of 60 or 145 or 200 or 300 members, conceptualize it as a federation of organizations that have a common meeting ground in the corporate worship of God, but each has its own distinctive identity, role, and purpose.

Typically these include the Sunday school, the women's organization, the youth group, the men's fellowship, and the ministry of music. Instead of planning how the congregation can reach more people, begin by asking each organization to develop its own growth strategy.

The key to implementing this strategy is a pastor who

(1) prefers to work with groups and organizations rather than with individuals on a one-to-one basis, (2) enjoys ambiguity and complexity, (3) accepts the responsibility for making worship the unifying thread in this mosaic, and (4) is comfortable with an eighteen- to twenty-four-month time frame for planning.

12. Build Large, Not Small, Groups

Consistent with this affirmation of the role of the various organizations is a related step. It begins with an affirmation of the role of large groups. Instead of attempting to build and nurture a network of small groups consisting of five to twelve people in each, the focus is on building large groups. Unless it is organized around a large cadre of trained, deeply committed, and dedicated volunteer leaders, the small group approach requires huge investments of paid staff time. If the staff is to be at the center of the group life, a reliance on large groups can reach many more people at a much lower cost. Unfortunately, this focus on large groups requires a far higher level of skill.[5]

In operational terms, this means organizing a chancel choir with 65 to 150 voices, Sunday school classes that range in size from 35 to 700, monthly meetings of the women's organization that attract at least 80 to 800 women, a youth program that includes at least five dozen teenagers, and 35 to 900 in the men's fellowship.

This can be a highly productive strategy for the congregation averaging 300 to 450 or more at worship. The price tag is a staff member with a high level of competence in creating and managing large groups and adequate meeting rooms for large groups.

13. Enhance the Spiritual Journey of People

One of the most widely followed and highly productive steps in recent years is to concentrate on meeting the spiritual needs of people.

This begins, of course, with preaching and worship, but also touches every other facet of parish life from the monthly meetings of the governing board to the teaching ministry to prayer cells to weekday Bible study groups to a strong affirmation of the power of intercessory prayer. The focus is on the yearnings or spiritual needs of people for hope, comfort, acceptance, community, and growth.

Obviously this requires a pastor with the appropriate gifts and priorities.

14. Build on Strengths

This often is a substantially different approach than the first step described in this chapter about carving out a niche. That step begins with identifying unmet needs and mobilizing the resources necessary to respond to that need.

This step begins with identifying the strengths, resources, assets, and distinctive traditions of this congregation. The next step is to affirm those strengths. The third is to identify the people who can be reached and served by those strengths and resources.

For smaller churches this often means a greater emphasis on responding to the personal and social needs of lonely people, of the recently widowed, of mature adults, and of people who live alone. That caring fellowship can be highly attractive!

The risk, of course, is if too many people respond, the spontaneity of that caring fellowship is eroded.

For many churches on a plateau, this step means identifying, affirming, and building on the strengths of the new pastor.

15. Change by Addition, Not Subtraction

Overlapping this last step is a simple and positive component of most strategies for planned change. Whenever possible, minimize disruption and threats to the status quo by avoiding change by subtraction. Do not dissolve a Sunday school class. Do not merge one circle in the women's organization into another aging and shrinking circle. Do not replace an existing program or group with a new one.

Always try to make changes by adding, but minimizing, any disturbance of the status quo. If the decision is made to add another worship service to the Sunday morning schedule, avoid changing the existing schedule. This may mean adding an early service at eight-thirty, rather than the preferred nine o'clock hour. It may mean asking a new adult class to meet in the house next door rather than dissolving that class of five who have been meeting in the same room for thirty years. It may mean two adult choirs every Sunday morning rather than trying to encourage young adults to join that chancel choir composed largely of people past fifty years of age. It may mean organizing a second high school age youth group rather than trying to change the existing group or replace the current volunteer leaders. This strategy is consistent with a policy of incremental rather than radical change.

16. Break the Spell of Passivity!

One of the most common reasons so many congregations settle down on a comfortable plateau in size, rather than seek to attract a substantial number of newcomers, is they have drifted into a passive stance. To a significant degree, this is a product of the Second Law of Thermodynamics. This basic law of physics declares that the energy put into an organization is never fully utilized for productive purposes. As time goes by, more and more energy is used to maintain the status quo.

In ecclesiastical terms this explains why the longer any one congregation has been meeting in the same building, the greater the difficulties it encounters in reaching and serving new generations of people. The natural tendency is for the members to grow old together as they grow smaller in numbers. One step off that plateau is to break that spell of passivity by redefining role or with new leadership or by a flood of new members.[6]

17. Identify the Barriers

This step begins with a careful, objective diagnostic effort to identify the barriers to growth. A reasonably competent and energetic mission development pastor can come into nearly any community on the North American continent and within six to ten months create a new congregation that includes at least two or three or four dozen adults. If this is possible, why cannot the existing congregations in that community reach those same people?

One part of the explanation may be the will to do it. Another may be passivity. A third is that most congregations unknowingly erect what outsiders perceive as barriers. The simplest, but far from rare, example is the advertisement in the newspaper or the Yellow Pages that lists the Sunday morning schedule. In fact, worship now begins a half hour earlier than advertised.

One beginning point is to take a group of people to another community on a Saturday morning and instruct them to walk around the exterior of two or three church buildings. The purpose is for them to identify the images conveyed to the complete stranger by that piece of real estate. The next step is for them to return home and walk around the exterior of our meeting place to identify the images we convey to strangers.

A parallel step is to ask several leaders to worship with another congregation next Sunday morning and identify the barriers they encountered. The barriers to strangers in your church will not be removed until after your leaders are convinced they exist.

18. Increase Redundancy!

The last of these steps that are least likely to threaten those who treasure continuity, stability, and predictability is based on a simple, but sound, set of assumptions. Four of them will illustrate the point.

1. Whatever you try will not produce a positive response from everyone.
2. Many messages are sent that are never received.
3. Many messages are received that were never sent.
4. Many good ideas are rejected the first time they are suggested.

For most churches on a plateau one of the most useful

steps is to increase the redundancy. The list of possibilities include a redundant system of internal communication between the congregation and the members, a redundant system for inviting outsiders to come here, a redundant system for making sure strangers receive a warm welcome, a redundant approach to youth ministries with several options offered to teenagers, designated second-mile giving to supplement the budget, two vacation Bible schools every summer, at least two services on Christmas Eve, at least three alternative approaches to Bible study, a redundant system for calling on first-time visitors, and a redundant system for enlisting volunteers.

An operational affirmation of redundancy can be a highly productive and relatively non-threatening step up off that plateau in size. It also can supplement and reinforce other strategies.

As you seek to help your congregation move up off that plateau in size, do you prefer to begin with a first step that affirms continuity or with a strategy that carries the price of substantial discontinuity with the past? In either case, it will be useful to review how you invite people to come to your church.

CHAPTER NINE

WHEN AND HOW DO WE INVITE?

What is the one area of ministry in which churches display their lowest level of effectiveness? What do churches do least well? Where is the greatest room for immediate improvement?

The answer clearly is not music or missions or community ministries or teaching stewardship or fellowship or worship or financial support of the clergy or constructing attractive and functional buildings. All of these have shown substantial improvement during the past sixty years. Some will argue the educational ministry has deteriorated. Others contend the quality of preaching has declined.

From this observer's perspective, the answer clearly is inviting outsiders to church. While improvements have been made by thousands of congregations, for most this is clearly the number-one weakness.

If that generalization is accepted, it introduces six steps that merit the attention of any congregation seeking to move up off a plateau in size.

Who?

The first of these six is to identify who will be invited and to agree on why they might come. The most useless response to that question is "We welcome everyone to come worship God with us. We refuse to discriminate among people, so we cannot narrow our invitation down to any one group."

If taken literally, this means that congregation is prepared to invite and welcome all six billion people on this planet. When that point was raised, one leader laughed and explained, "No, what we mean is we are prepared to welcome everyone who lives within a reasonable driving time of our church."

That raised two questions. First, what is a reasonable driving time? Ten minutes? Thirty minutes? Forty minutes? An hour? Second, that congregation meets in a building that is within thirty minutes' driving time of 100,000 residents. Since the nave seats only 400, the best they could do would be to accommodate fewer than 3,000 in seven or eight worship services on any one weekend. They are not prepared to welcome 10,000 people, much less 100,000. They also are not prepared to offer people the choice among even three different worship experiences.

More important, how will they invite 100,000 people? That brings us back to the first step. Who will be invited and why will they come? A few minutes' thought will produce several qualifications. First, the vast majority of Protestant congregations on the North American continent are prepared to welcome only those who want to worship in English, who are not hearing impaired, who are not seeking the traditional Roman Catholic mass, who would find our style of corporate worship to be meaningful, who are free to attend church on Sunday morning, who are able to transport themselves to our meeting place, who will find our music to be acceptable, who will be comfortable with the way we dress for church, who can walk up steps, and who will not come in such huge numbers that no room will be left for our own members who may arrive a minute late. Those qualifications reduce that 100,000 to several hundred or fewer.

A far better beginning point is to forget that nonsense about welcoming everyone and to identify a manageable number. The historic approach, which is now largely obsolete, was to concentrate on the people who lived within a mile or two of the meeting place. In today's mobile society, in which the place of residence often is unrelated to the place of work or the place of recreation or the place of retail shopping or the place of worship, this tends to produce more frustration than results. The one big exception is the neighborhood-oriented vacation Bible school for children.

The most productive approach begins with a question: What are the religious and personal needs of today's population that we are prepared to respond to in a meaningful way? To use what some consider to be an obscene word, what is our market? What is the one area of ministry in which the churches display their lowest level of effectiveness? What do the churches do least well? Where is the greatest room for immediate improvement?

Are we seeking to reach and serve those who prefer the intimacy and spontaneity of the small church? Those who want inspiring expository preaching? Those who want a superb choir? Those who prefer a liberal interpretation of the Bible? Those who seek a literal interpretation? Those who want a big youth ministry filled with many choices for teenagers? Those who are looking for a strong missions focus? Those who want to be challenged to be engaged in doing ministry? Those who come seeking a message of love, comfort, and hope? Newlyweds seeking to meet and make friends with other young married couples? Parents who want a Christian day school for their children? Families with a physically handicapped member? Those who want a truly racially integrated fellowship? Those who want to worship in Korean? Mature adults who want a seven-day-a-week program to fill their empty days? Those who are seeking a big church filled with attractive choices that also affirms anonymity? Those who long for a place in a small and intimate caring community?

Only a handful of congregations can authentically respond, "Yes, we can meet all those expectations except two."

Thus for nearly all churches, the first step is to identify in reasonably precise terms the wants and needs that this parish is prepared to meet.

The Prospect List

The logical next step is to build a list of prospective future members. This list consists of the names and addresses of people who might decide to make this their new church home. This list includes the self-motivated first-time visitors; the non-member parents of children enrolled in the Sunday school and last summer's vacation Bible school; names of friends, neighbors, and colleagues at work suggested by members; new residents in that community; new parents; people who have turned to this church in the recent past for weddings, funerals, and ministerial services; non-members who attended here on Christmas Eve last year; and others.

At a minimum that list will include at least one-half as many names as are carried on the membership roster.

Thus the 400-member congregation will have at least 200 names on the prospect list. As the months roll by and new sources of names are utilized, that list should become as long as the membership roster.

When?

After the list of prospective future members includes a substantial number of names, the time has come to move to the third step in this six-part sequence: When will these prospective future members be invited to come to your church?

For churches that are on a plateau in size or that are shrinking in numbers, Sunday morning worship probably should rank no higher than nineteenth on that list. Why? One obvious reason is if Sunday morning worship was the number-one asset, that congregation probably would be growing in numbers. (At this point the reader may want to put down this book and examine the church advertisements in the Friday or Saturday edition of the local newspaper. Most, if not all, of those ads focus on Sunday morning. If that is true in your community, do you want to compete with what these other churches see as their strongest attraction? Or do you want to lift up a unique asset or a specialized ministry?) One exception to that generalization may be when you are welcoming a new pastor. This may be the time to invite people to come and help pioneer a new era in your congregation's history with this newly arrived minister. A second exception is those congregations seeking to reach adults born before 1940. As a group, this generation tends to make their initial contact with their new church home on Sunday morning.

In summary, this third step requires a choice between a first priority and a second priority. Will the first priority be given to inviting potential new members to come for the first time on Sunday morning? Or will the first priority be given to another time?

If you enjoy the preaching of a minister who excels in both sermon content and delivery and/or if you have a superb chancel choir and/or if you are organizing two or more new adult Sunday school classes and/or if you offer a lively, moving, and highly spiritual worship experience that is strong on visual communication, you probably should concentrate your efforts on inviting people to come on Sunday morning. (If you contend you score high on all four of those variables and are still on a plateau in size, you have other problems that are beyond the scope of this book!)

What?

If you now have many names on the prospect list, but you have agreed Sunday morning should not be the primary focus of your invitations, what are the alternatives? That is the fourth step in this process.

The best response is to call on every person on that prospect list as part of an effort to surface needs to which your church can respond.

The second best response is to look at what has worked for other churches and to choose those possibilities that match your resources and local situations. That list may include inviting people to (1) worship with you on Christmas Eve, (2) help pioneer a new afternoon program of structured socializing experiences for children who are being educated at home by their parents, (3) share in the creation of a new Mothers' Club, (4) attend

your vacation Bible school, (5) join a new church soft-
ball team, (6) be charter members of a new women's
Bible study group that meets every Thursday afternoon,
(7) share in a men's Saturday morning Bible study and
prayer group, (8) help pioneer a new mutual support
group your congregation is organizing, (9) enroll their
children in a one-day-a-week after-school program from
4:00 to 7:30 P.M., (10) join a women's prayer circle, (11)
volunteer to help staff an ongoing community ministry
such as sheltering the homeless or feeding the hungry or
visiting residents of a nursing home, (12) help pioneer
the new Saturday evening worship service your congregation is preparing to offer, (13) join a drama group your
congregation is organizing in order to put on a particular
play, (14) help design a cooperative Parents' Day Out
program your congregation will soon offer, (15) enroll
their young children in a new music encounter group
that meets every Tuesday, (16) encourage parents to urge
their teenagers to join your youth group, (17) worship
with you during a series of Holy Week evening services,
(18) enroll in a divorce recovery event sponsored by your
congregation, or (19) pioneer the creation of a new par-
ents-of-twins group.

That list is far from exhaustive. It is offered to suggest a
range of possibilities for weekday events to which potential future members may be invited. The crucial point is
that most of those nineteen possibilities share one common characteristic: help pioneer the new.

How?

The safest assumption for this fifth step is that whatever you try as a channel for inviting people will be less

than fully effective. In other words, this step requires persistence, patience, redundancy, variety, creativity, and money.

A modest goal is that at least 2 percent of the total annual financial expenditures will be allocated to inviting people to come to your church. If you are serious and/or in a highly competitive ecclesiastical environment, that figure probably should be closer to 5 percent.

The crucial point, however, is not how much money is spent on advertising. The crucial point is that the quality and relevance of the first-time visitor's experience will motivate that visitor to want to return. Too many churches waste money on newspaper and Yellow Page ads inviting people to come to Sunday morning worship, but most first-time visitors depart convinced, "Well, I learned one thing this morning. This is not the church for me. I'm not coming back here again!"

That is why this "How?" step follows after that "What?" question. For most congregations, direct mail,[1] television (if you have a pastor who is perceived as an attractive personality by the television audience and who also is an excellent visual communicator), radio, newspaper ads (if they focus on the needs of the reader rather than on the church's schedule or institutional identity), the Yellow Pages, and door hangers are among the second-best channels for inviting people to come to your church.

The best, of course, is face-to-face personal invitations by the pastor, the staff, and trained volunteers.

In either case the initial focus should be on the other person's needs, not on what the church has to offer.[2]

What If?

Many leaders fear that no one will respond, so they are reluctant to undertake an aggressive effort to invite people. The real risk is what if people do respond? This leads to the sixth step. It includes a half dozen components.

First, the event or program or service or ministry to which strangers are invited should be designed to welcome non-members, to help them feel they were expected, and to cause them to depart feeling glad they came.

Second, a redundant follow-up system should be in place. This may include a visit from the pastor, a letter, a telephone call, a visit from a volunteer, and an invitation to return for a subsequent event, program, service, or ministry.

Third, if these contacts so indicate, their names go on your permanent mailing list.

Fourth, any member of that household who did not attend the first event should receive invitations to what may meet their needs.

Fifth, as a part of those initial visits by the pastor and/or volunteers, these prospective future members are invited to express their hopes, wishes, and expectations about what they seek in a church.

Finally, their names remain on the prospect list until (a) they ask that they be removed or (b) they have joined another church or (c) at least five additional face-to-face visits or contacts have been completed.

Persistence is one of the essential components of a strategy to move up off that plateau in size. That includes persistence in following up on first-time visitors who respond to an invitation.

CHAPTER TEN

FOUR RADICAL CHANGES

It is almost impossible to overstate the difficulties long-established congregations face as they seek to move up off a plateau in size or to reverse a long period of numerical decline. Most of those that do experience a substantial increase in numbers usually combine the three steps (improvement in quality, a meaningful response to the religious needs of people, and a highly productive staff) identified in chapter 4.

A more modest growth pattern can be found in those churches that implement several of the other three dozen steps described in chapters 2, 3, 5, 6, 7, 8, and 9. The most discouraging fact is that the majority of Protestant congregations in North America that (1) were established before 1960 and/or (2) have been meeting in the same building at the same location for at least thirty years and/or (3) have been on a plateau in size or slowly shrinking in numbers for at least seven years follow one of three paths. The most attractive of the three is they continue on that plateau. The second is they shrink in size. The third is they disappear either by dissolution or by merging into another congregation.

This dismal record is not cited to discourage those who are determined to make their church an exception to that general pattern. It is cited to introduce what many will perceive to be radical proposals for change.

These four strategies, while they differ sharply in substance, share four common characteristics.

1. Each represents a radical departure from the status quo.
2. Each usually arouses widespread initial opposition.
3. Each one, if carefully implemented, can be a road to substantial numerical growth.
4. Each one requires changes that are very difficult to reverse and return to "the way it used to be here."

When Relocation Is Rejected

One of the seven steps described in chapter 8 that results in great discontinuity with the past is the relocation of the meeting place. This can be an exceptionally effective means of moving the tradition-bound congregation into a new chapter in its history. From a denominational perspective, it ranks third behind planting new churches and encouraging the emergence of more large congregations as the three most valuable components of a church-growth strategy. Every denomination should consider encouraging one percent of all long-established congregations to relocate their meeting place in any given year.

The most common drawback to relocation is that it is almost always rejected the first time it is presented at a congregational meeting. One reason may be that relocation was brought to a vote before all the necessary advance work had been completed. A second, of course, is it represents great discontinuity with the past. (Those who define the church as a gathered people find relocation easier to support than do those who define the church as a sacred place. Therefore relocation always should be presented as a proposal to relocate the meeting place, not to relocate the congregation.)

Another reason the relocation proposal usually is rejected when first presented is the wording of the motion. A typical generic proposal is Do you favor (a) continuing to meet at this location or (b) relocating the meeting place to a new site? This wording loads the question in favor of the status quo.

If those proposing relocation are convinced the status quo is *not* a viable option, the wording should reflect that judgment and not offer the status quo as a viable option. Thus one choice could be Do you favor (a) merging with another congregation or (b) relocating our meeting place? A different choice could be Do you favor (a) relocation or (b) a continued aging and shrinkage in the size of this congregation?

For the purpose of this discussion the question would be stated in these terms: Do you favor (a) relocating our meeting place and disposing of this property or (b) becoming a multi-site congregation with two meeting places?

In other words, if relocation appears to be the most attractive step up off that plateau in size, the compromise could be a "both-and" alternative. Today at least 400, and perhaps as many as 800, Protestant congregations have chosen this course of action. They now function as one congregation with one governing board, one staff, one budget, one comprehensive program, one membership roster, one set of committees, one treasury, one treasurer, and one set of internally consistent and coherent ministry goals. The two distinctive characteristics are (a) they own and operate two or more meeting places and (b) they attract more new members year after year than they lose. A few also have two sets of trustees, one for each place.

The pastor or the senior minister preaches at both locations at least forty Sunday mornings every year, a full Sunday school is held at each place, and congregation-wide events (the annual congregational meeting, the monthly meeting of the governing board, etc.) rotate from one site to the other.

While many members initially express considerable skepticism, this can be a productive road to take. It is far more likely to be a meaningful course of action than waiting passively for a miracle to happen. It also may be a more productive course of action than spending a decade or longer persuading members to dispose of this property and construct a new building on a new site.

From Sunday Morning to Seven Days a Week

Most of the Protestant congregations on the North American continent that averaged 350 or more at worship in 1955 have followed one of five paths. The least numerous are those that have continued on a plateau in size for the following four decades. The largest number have taken the path of numerical decline. A modest number have disappeared from the scene, either by merging into another congregation or by dissolution. A fourth group have chosen to make a fresh start by relocating the meeting place. (A few of those have become multi-site churches.) The fifth group consists of those that have been transformed from a Sunday church, in which most of the participants come rarely except on Sunday, to a seven-day-a-week-program church.[1] The number of people participating in a program, ministry, event, group, class, worship experience, or gathering during the week is nearly equal to, and may exceed, the number of people who appear on Sunday morning or Sunday morning and Sunday evening combined.

Implementation of this concept requires a radical redefinition of the primary role of the staff (from taking care of today's members to building program), of the priorities on the time, talents, and energy of volunteers (from administration to ministry), and of the self-image of that congregation (from a neighborhood parish to a regional church).

Why is it a promising step for the congregation seeking to move up off the plateau in size? First, this design forces the leaders to focus on the needs of people rather than on the tradition of what this church always has offered people. It requires a shift from a producer-of-services perspective to the needs-of-consumers orientation. Second, it creates countless attractive new entry points for potential future members. Third, most volunteers find that emphasis in ministry to be more rewarding than the focus on administration. Fourth, a responsiveness to the contemporary needs of people is more likely to spark creativity than is an effort to perpetuate tradition.

Incidentally, this general trend of more of the larger churches shifting to seven-day-a-week programing is one part of the explanation for the fact that today approximately 15 percent of all Protestant congregations account for at least two-thirds of all adults who choose a new church home in the typical month. This is one reason why the big are getting bigger and the small are becoming smaller.

Take a Big Leap!

"Last year we averaged 88 in Sunday morning worship, that was up from 86 a year earlier, but down from 91 ten years ago and 90 five years ago," reflected a longtime member. "My wish is that five years from now we'll be averaging somewhere between 130 and 150. That would give us the financial base we need to pay our bills; we would have enough volunteers to fill all the slots; we should be able to attract and keep a top quality pastor; and maybe we could go to a closely graded Sunday school."

"You're too modest," objected the recently arrived pastor. "My dream is that in five years this congregation will be averaging at least 250 in worship and we'll have at least 200 in the Sunday school every week. I hope that within seven years we'll be a full-service church averaging at least 350 in worship."

"That's too big!" replied the veteran member. "You're talking about nearly tripling the size of our congregation. That would mean we would have to go to two services on Sunday morning, build several more classrooms, and add a lot more staff to the payroll. That's more change than I think most of our people are ready to take. I prefer more modest goals. Why do you want us to grow so much so fast?"

"Several reasons," explained the new pastor. "First, of course, is the Great Commission that Jesus gave us. Second, the potential for that kind of growth is here. The fields are white for the harvest. Third, we own five acres of land, so we could easily quadruple in size on this site. Fourth, I'm convinced this congregation has a lot to offer people, and we're only beginning to tap our potential. Fifth, I've seen too many congregations grow rather modestly under one pastor and then slip back to their former size a few years after the arrival of the next minister. I want to institutionalize a new role, a new self-image, a new community image, and a new approach to ministry here before I leave so that can't happen!"

This brief conversation illustrates the difference between modest incremental change and transformational change. The veteran leader wished this congregation could continue much as it is, with only a modest growth in numbers. The new pastor seeks to transform the identity and role of this parish.

The veteran leader wants to break through one barrier in size and move up to a new plateau in size. While not stated in these terms, that leader's wish is to move from one comfortable plateau in size up to the next comfortable plateau in size. The new minister hopes to break through two barriers in size and move up and through that next comfortable plateau in which the average worship attendance is in the 125 to 175 bracket into a new and radically different style of congregational life.[2]

The bold goal is to transform this congregation into a full service, seven-day-a-week-program church that can respond to the religious and personal needs of two or three or four generations of people. The modest goal is to keep everything the same, except to include more people. Which of the two is more likely to move this congregation up off that plateau and keep it there?

Expand the Choices!

A common characteristic of most congregations, regardless of size, that are on a plateau or shrinking in size is that they offer people two choices: Take it or leave it. This usually includes one adult choir; one youth group for high school students; one annual financial appeal; one preacher on any given Sunday; one adult Sunday school class for any one age cohort; one Sunday school class for fourth graders; one approach to the corporate worship of

God (if two services are scheduled for Sunday morning, they will be carbon copies and the only choice is the hour); one room for worship; one women's organization with every circle organized around study, fellowship, and mission;[3] one week of vacation Bible school each summer; one Bible study group that meets during the week; and one service on Christmas Eve.

The unspoken message is "This is it! Accept what we offer, or go somewhere else." For many, the big expansion of choices in recent years was a choice between parking on the street or parking in the church-owned lot—if you arrive before it is filled. Perhaps a second change was that you can now enter the building from either the parking lot in the rear or the street entrance.

The desire to expand that range of choices can be an effective step up off the plateau in size, but frequently it is viewed as excessive change by those who prefer the alternatives of take it or leave it.

Where do you begin? That will depend on the local variables, but the possibilities are endless. It may be by designing two or three or four different Christmas Eve services, each directed at a clearly defined audience. (The first may be a four o'clock "Birthday Party for Jesus" designed for young children and the last an eleven o'clock service designed for young adults without children.)

An increasingly popular one is to offer two different worship services every Sunday morning with two different adult choirs (one for the early service and one for the late service). In larger congregations this can be expanded by scheduling one minister to preach at the early service forty-five Sundays a year and the other minister (or a lay preacher) at the second service. This can be supplemented by one set of hymns for the first hour and a differ-ent set for the second service.

Another is to schedule two vacation Bible schools—one in late June and the other in early August. In each the number-one goal is to reach newcomers to that com-munity, but volunteers have a choice as to when they will work. The children may choose the one that does not conflict with family vacation plans, or they may enroll in both.

The clearest need for choices is based on the assump-tion that no one youth group is likely to interest more than one-half of today's teenagers, so two (or three or four) different youth groups, each with its own set of adult volunteer leaders, are organized.

The obvious benefit is the opportunity to appeal to a larger number of people by responding to a broader range of needs. Equally significant, however, is the fact that this can be (this is not automatic) the first step in changing from a producer orientation to a consumer orientation. The big fringe benefit, of course, is the larger the number and variety of choices, the larger the number of attractive entry points. This alternative of sharply increasing the range of choices can be the most promising step up off that plateau for congregations that now average between 145 and 700 at worship. It also may turn out to be so threatening that it will not win the support necessary for implementation. It is an especially appropriate step for the congregation composed largely of people born before 1940 who seek to reach and serve those born after 1955. Which of these four radical steps would be appropriate for your congregation?

CHAPTER ELEVEN

GROWING WITH GROWTH

For years, maybe a decade or two, we averaged between 80 and 95 at Sunday morning church," recalled a longtime member of a congregation founded in 1903 in a town that now includes nearly 7,000 residents. "Then about twenty years ago we got a young hotshot preacher who came in and got everybody enthused. He turned out not only to be the best preacher in town, but he also really knew how to motivate people. Pretty soon our church attendance was setting new records, and we had to go to two services. The Sunday school grew so much we had to build that eight-room addition on the west side of the church. We also bought and tore down two old houses next door to the church to provide more parking. He was by far the best minister I've ever known. When he left after about eight years, we were averaging close to 300 at worship, we had a full-time associate, and the Sunday school was twice as big as it had been when he came."

"What happened next?" inquired the visitor.

"Oh, some big church in Ohio came and made him an offer he couldn't refuse and we couldn't match, so he left. Now we're back down to about 85 or 90 in church on the typical Sunday. The Sunday school has shrunk to the point we don't need all the space, so we rent out five rooms in the new wing to a woman here in town who runs a nursery school. She uses one room for her office and supplies and has classes five days a week in the other four. The rent she pays covers the utilities plus one-half the monthly payments on that twenty-year mortgage we took out to pay for it." This brief account, which could be replicated in countless churches, illustrates three points. The obvious one is the potential impact of the skilled leader who displays a winsome personality, is an excellent preacher, is a productive worker, is an excellent theological match for that particular congregation, and can rally support for challenging goals. A second point is that rapid numerical growth may not be permanent. The more that growth is built around the personality of one person, the more likely that many people will disappear shortly after the departure of that magnetic personality.

Growth or Change?

A third, and more subtle, point is the distinction between making changes and institutionalizing a new era. A fourteen-year-old boy's first date may mark the beginning of a new era in that young man's life, but it is not the same as getting married. Taking a girl to a rock concert is not the same as going on a honeymoon with a new wife. An experience is not the same as a commitment.

The congregation described here experienced, for eight exciting years, the leadership of a venturesome, creative, and energetic pastor. The people, however, apparently did not make a commitment to a new role in ministry. That parish experienced temporary change, but it was not transformed into a new creation.

The distinction between change and transformation represents the most crucial of the 44 steps described in

this book. It is one thing to move up off a plateau in size
for a period of time. That is not the same as adopting and
implementing a completely different style of congregational life. It is one thing for a resident of Manhattan,
Kansas, to visit New York City for a few days. It is a radically different experience to move from Kansas to New
York City.

The congregation described here, with the leadership
of an exceptionally competent tour guide, made an eight-
year visit to a fast paced and exciting world. When that
tour guide departed, they returned to a familiar, comfortable, and slower paced life.

This distinction between growing larger and changing
is complicated by the tendency of most church members
to hope for growth without change. "We would like to
continue pretty much as we are, except have more people" summarizes that widespread wish.

A central thesis of this book is that moving up off that
plateau to either (a) a new plateau in size that includes
more people or (b) continued long-term numerical
growth carries a price tag. That price tag is change. That
experience can be summarized by the frequently heard
reflection, "It's not the same here as it used to be."

To be more specific, institutionalizing a growth strategy
carries many different price tags. Among the most common are these eight.

1. The most widely neglected of these eight price tags
on a permanent move up off that plateau in size is the
need to assimilate newcomers.[1] Few congregations have
built in an ongoing, self-winding, and effective system for
the assimilation of new members.

One reason for this is that the longtime member and
the current leaders, most of whom are completely assimi-

lated, feel no need for it. A second reason, which was illustrated by the congregation described earlier in this chapter, is that in many congregations the newcomers build a relationship with the pastor that creates the illusion they have been fully assimilated. When that magnetic personality departs, they discover they are not a part of the fellowship. A third reason is the difference between attractive entry points and a process for the assimilation of new people. The drama group that works together intensively for three months to produce a play once a year can be a highly attractive entry point. A week after the last performance, however, that entry point closes for another nine months. Where will that newcomer find a permanent home in the larger fellowship? A similar experience may await the newcomer who is a hardworking volunteer in the vacation Bible school. That entry point ceases to exist as a place for assimilation a week or two after it opened. The failure to pay this price for numerical growth frequently evokes this comment, "Yeah, we're getting a lot of new members through the front door, but we're losing almost as many out the back door."

2. The faster the rate of numerical growth, the more likely it will be accompanied by an increase in the pace of congregational life. This can be disconcerting to those longtime members who enjoy a slower pace. One of the most effective means of reversing that pattern of numerical growth and moving back down to a lower plateau in size is for the next pastor to be a low energy person who prefers a slower pace. This ministerial style also can win quick support from those who were unhappy with the consequences of rapid growth.

3. A rapid rate of numerical growth, an increase in the number and variety of attractive entry points for newcom-

ers, and the greater the degree of redundancy in the process for the assimilation of new people, the more likely that moving up off a plateau will mean an increase in complexity. This increase in the complexity of congregational life usually is reflected in the schedule, the organizational structure, the decision-making processes, the use of the building, and in the relationships among the staff as well as the relationships of the staff with the governing board.

Since most people prefer simplicity to complexity, considerable resistance may surface to paying this price.

4. For many longtime members, and especially the older ones, the most visible and most irksome price tag on moving up off that comfortable plateau is the increase in anonymity.

American society includes two unwritten, but widely followed, rules. The first is that younger people are expected to learn and remember the names of older people, but older people are not expected to remember the names of younger people. The second is that newcomers are expected to learn and remember the names of longtime members, but longtime members are not expected to remember the names of newcomers.

Thus a natural and predictable price tag on a strategy to grow larger and younger is an increase in anonymity.

5. The combination of these first four price tags on numerical growth creates a fifth. This is the need for better internal communication between the parish as an institution and the individual members. The increase in the pace of congregational life means the monthly newsletter must become a weekly with a clear future orientation. The increase in anonymity means the grapevine no longer is a reliable channel for internal communica-

tion. The rise in complexity requires greater redundancy in the internal communication network. The need to assimilate newcomers requires both more messages and more precisely worded messages. One of the effective components of a strategy to reduce the size of a large and growing parish is to cut back on that internal communication system and/or to fill it with errors.

6. Not only is greater redundancy required in the internal communication network, but that is a price tag of growth. This includes more redundancy in the ministries with teenagers, in hospital visitation, in financial appeals, in the teaching ministry, in the schedule, in the ministry of music, and in staffing.

Redundant systems represent one cost of reaching more people. All we know for certain is that no one system, program, class, group, event, ministry, choir, or worship service will meet the needs of everyone. The cost of increased redundancy is one reason unit costs rise as the size of the congregation increases.

7. Another basic generalization is that as size goes up, quality becomes more important. Kinship and fellowship ties, the attachment to this sacred place, local traditions, inherited loyalties, habit, guilt, and the feeling of "I'll be missed if I don't go, so I guess I'd better go" are still powerful motivating factors for continued participation with many of today's adults from the generations born before 1940. They also are powerful motivating forces for long-time members in smaller churches.

Those congregations seeking to move up off a plateau in size and/or to reach, attract, serve, and assimilate newcomers in general, and especially the generations born after 1955, must place a greater emphasis on quality as a motivating force for participation. Thus permanent enhancement in quality is a price tag for staying on that higher plateau in size, for attracting a continuing stream of newcomers, and for retaining the allegiance of the people.

8. From a pastor's perspective, the number-one price tag is represented by the change in the minister's role.[2] More time is spent with groups of people and less with individuals. Ambiguity replaces predictability. Discontinuity is more common than continuity. The pace of people coming and going doubles or triples from what it was when that congregation was on a plateau in size. The year replaces the month as the basic time frame for planning. Instead of reacting to events, surprises, and the initiatives of others, the pastor gladly accepts the role of an initiating leader. More time must be reserved for sermon preparation and less for one-to-one relationships.

Instead of "doing it," the pastor is expected "to make sure it happens." Instead of attempting to do everything, the pastor specializes in what he or she can do best. The contemporary religious needs of people replaces local traditions as the beginning point for planning ministry. The average hour now has to yield forty or fifty minutes of productive time, not ten or twenty. The congregation must be conceptualized as a passing parade of groups, classes, people, choirs, circles, cells, task forces, and officers, not as a permanent collection of individuals. Wisdom surpasses academic credentials on the list of valuable personal qualifications. That congregation, not the denomination, becomes the number-one institutional reference point for the pastor. The professional network with the senior pastors of other large and growing congregations replaces the network of ministers in the local regional judicatory.

Although that is far from an exhaustive list, those are among the price tags for the pastor in a permanent move up off a plateau in size.

How critical are these eight price tags? That can be illustrated by returning to the congregation described earlier in this chapter. Why did it drop back off that higher plateau in size?

One reason was identified earlier. Most of the people in the flood of new members joined the pastor. They were not assimilated into the fellowship of the parish. When that pastor departed, their church closed.

Second, the successor pastor was a low energy, relaxed, non-directive individual who slowed the pace of congregational life. This was welcomed and affirmed by many of the old timers.

Third, with the support of all who preferred simplicity to complexity, the Sunday morning schedule was reduced to one service, and several cutbacks in programing were made. Part of the context for this was an agreement to not replace the departed associate minister in order to save money. A related economy move initiated by the new pastor was to return to a monthly schedule for the newsletter. This followed the departure of the associate minister who was the editor of the weekly newsletter. The desire to simplify life also reduced the level of redundancy.

Finally, the new minister came after nine years as the pastor of a congregation that had been averaging 85 to 90 at worship. The easy, comfortable, and, to some extent, predictable course of action for this fifty-five-year-old minister was to encourage the congregation to fit his ministerial style rather than to change his style to fit the needs of this fast-paced, growing, and dynamic parish.

That decision was strongly affirmed by many longtime members who also placed a high value on one-to-one relationships with the pastor. ("Our new minister is so much more approachable, and he never seems to be in a hurry to get away when you're talking to him.") These members also appreciated the slower pace, less complexity, and greater intimacy. These members also shared the new minister's positive feelings about stability, predictability, continuity with the past, and economizing wherever possible in expenditures.

The vast majority of members will vote in favor of a strategy to move up off the current plateau in size. Far fewer are willing to pay the price required for a permanent spot on that higher plateau in size.

Growing with growth is an essential component of any plan to avoid falling back down in size.

CHAPTER TWELVE

WHAT IF IT DOES (NOT) WORK?

Sooner or later the leaders in every congregation that seeks to move up off a plateau in size will endure one of two stress-producing experiences. (That may be sufficient reason to ignore this book and continue to relax on a comfortable plateau.)

The more common of the two is the frustration expressed in the words, "We tried it, but it didn't work for us. If it works for other churches, why did we fail?"

The less common is a product of success. "We did exactly what was suggested, and our congregation has nearly doubled in size in five years. We're happy with that, but no one warned us about all the unanticipated surprises, changes, adjustments, and disruptions we've experienced."

Both reactions are natural, normal, and predictable. Both have been experienced by the leaders in many other churches.

What Went Wrong?

The temptation to define the lack of success as failure is all too common. Frequently that is a misleading conclusion. A wiser and more productive course of action would be to step back and ask what went wrong. Why did the results not match or at least not come close to our expectations? What did we learn that can improve our ministry?

Careful postmortems of scores of unsuccessful efforts by congregations to move up off a plateau in size reveal at least a dozen recurring themes. It is not uncommon for more than one of these themes to surface in a single postmortem.

1. Perhaps the most widespread problem is a product of excessive impatience. The leaders who designed the strategy become so convinced they have identified both the heart of the problem and the ideal solution that they move too fast. Typically the decision to call a congregational meeting to approve what clearly is the wise, logical, rational, appropriate, and necessary course of action came too early. Instead of receiving the necessary approval, the proposal was voted down.

Rather than pause to analyze what had happened and to design a better process, the leaders concluded this negative vote represented final and irrevocable rejection.

This is especially common with proposals to relocate the meeting place. The recommendations for rapid change and sharp discontinuity with the past usually are rejected the first couple of times they are proposed. It helps if that is viewed as normal, natural, and predictable behavior in the process of planned change, rather than as permanent rejection.

2. A second theme is that this was not the appropriate strategy for that congregation at that point in its history. A different beginning point or a different strategy might have been adopted and fully implemented. Perhaps the most common example of that is when a proposal is made

to implement a high commitment strategy in what really is a low commitment parish.

This same pattern appears in capital funds campaigns, proposals to increase the frequency of worship attendance by members, or to double the number of teenagers who are active in the youth program. If this is the heart of the issue, the best beginning point probably is to (a) choose another strategy or (b) devote five years to raising the commitment level of the members.

3. An all-too-common reason the dream was not fulfilled is that the pastor moved prematurely. Any decision to move up off that plateau in size should be accompanied by a commitment by the current pastor to stay until the program has been fully implemented and the new era has become the new status quo. (The obvious exception, of course, is when replacement of the current pastor is the central component of the new strategy!)

4. Another common barrier to a successful implementation of the strategy is the shortage of program staff. Occasionally, this is simply an inadequate number of paid program staff members. More frequently, the crucial point is the strategy requires a highly productive staff and the present staff rates a 2 or 3 on the productivity scale of 1 to 6. The most common facet of this problem, however, is that the strategy requires a high level of specialized competence and the staff is composed entirely of generalists. Occasionally the staff attempt to single-handedly implement a design that calls for large numbers of carefully selected, thoroughly trained, and deeply committed volunteers.

5. Another source of frustration and disappointment comes with the painful surprise that the physical facilities cannot accommodate the new program.

One example is when the Sunday morning church averaging 500 at worship decides to become a seven-day-a-week program parish. The parking needed to accommodate 300 vehicles is available on Sunday morning, but most of it is not owned by that congregation. It is not available to accommodate 200 to 300 people for daytime programing or 300 to 500 for weeknight events. A second common example is the building designed to accommodate 500 people at worship, 80 people in adult classes, and 100 at a dinner in the fellowship hall.

A second example is a product of the fact that as size goes up, the demand for higher quality also rises. Space is available for eight adult classes. The three small classes that do exist choose the best rooms. When five new large classes are added, people begin to stay away because the quality of the rooms does not meet their expectations.

6. A fairly common barrier to moving up off a plateau surfaces when a handful of visionary, enthusiastic, committed, eager, creative, naive, venturesome, and energetic leaders decide to make moving up off that plateau the top priority They discover they have severely limited support. Why? The vast majority of the members are completely absorbed in what their leaders identify as a means-to-an-end or institutional survival issue.

In real life, it rarely is possible to implement ministry or identity goals when survival goals dominate people's thinking. That explains why resolving internal disputes, paying the bills, and taking care of the real estate are listed as the second, third, and fourth potential steps in the second part of chapter 8.

7. Another disruption to the implementation of a growth strategy may come when the key volunteer leader (a) moves away; (b) becomes heavily involved in family,

business, or personal concerns outside that parish; (c) decides another issue should be the current top priority in that congregation's life; or (d) encounters a moral crisis.

A common example may be when that key volunteer goes away for a few days to an inspiring event focused on the urgency of world missions. When that leader returns, the goal of reaching more people locally may be perceived as self-centered, parochial, and insignificant when compared to the urgency of carrying the gospel to all parts of the world.

8. Too often enthusiasm, impatience, and the clarity of the vision encourage the leaders to believe it will be easy to mobilize all the resources (volunteers, money, votes, program priorities, energy, staff time) that will be necessary to implement the strategy. At the congregational meeting, the vote is overwhelmingly in favor of the proposal. Four months later, these leaders discover this was not a vote of support, but rather permission "for you to make all of this happen without involving us."

9. Sometimes the dream exceeds the resources.

One example is the proposal to make a personal visit on every home within two miles of the meeting place, but only five people volunteer to make those calls. A second is the decision to organize two new adult Bible study groups or Sunday school classes annually, but only one qualified person volunteers to organize and teach a new class. A third is when a planning committee recommends a $500,000 plan to improve the real estate, but only $180,000 is raised in the capital funds appeal.

10. Occasionally a strategy is chosen that requires more energy, time, competence, commitment, or skill than the present pastor can or will provide.

11. In at least a few congregations a relatively small initiating group of deeply committed people chose the

appropriate next steps in a strategy to move up off that plateau—but that strategy requires more resources than that small group can mobilize.

12. In other churches the necessary volunteers were interested, supportive, willing, available, and enthusiastic—but no one thought to provide the training experiences required for these volunteers to master the necessary skills for designing and implementing that proposed new course of action.

Common examples include a failure to train volunteers for visitation-evangelism or for teaching in an expanded Sunday school or for nurturing the small group life or for developing new ministries with teenagers or for opening a Christian day school or for offering a ministry with developmentally disabled adults or for changing from a focus on small groups to large groups.

One response to these and similar disappointments is to abandon the goal of moving up off that plateau in size. A more productive response begins with the question "What did we learn that will enable us to do better next time?"

What If It Does Work?

When a congregation that has been on a plateau in size for several years decides to move up off that plateau, four outcomes are possible. One is the effort does not fulfill expectations. The logical next step is not to give up, but rather to conduct the postmortem suggested in the first pages of this chapter.

A second possibility is limited or partial success. Modest growth does come, but it is not sufficient to force the leaders to redefine the role and to reshape the style of ministry to undergird that new role.

A third, and far too common, possibility is that within several years that congregation slips back down off that plateau. Eight common explanations were discussed in the previous chapter.

The fourth possibility is either the emergence of a new and permanent role on a new plateau that includes serving many more people or, less frequently, unending and continuing numerical growth. Either of these two variations of long-term and permanent change often produces unanticipated consequences. Several of these—such as greater complexity, increased anonymity, and the need for more redundancy—were discussed in the previous chapter. Five others deserve a brief word here.

A common surprise is the unanticipated departure of a few longtime members who were overwhelmed by the changes, the faster pace, and the other price tags. They conclude it would be easier either to find a new church home or simply to drop out of church altogether rather than to adapt to that new world. It is not uncommon for some of them to continue to participate in a group (Sunday school class social events, circle in the women's organization, or service group) in which they have many longtime friends.

The closest to a guaranteed consequence of becoming a larger congregation is a rise in unit costs. In 1992 the numerically growing congregation now averaging 450 at worship on Sunday morning typically spent five or six times as much money, not three times as much, as the congregation averaging 150 at worship. Size, choices, and quality cost money! This often is a great disappointment to those who had hoped a large increase in members would result in only a modest increase in the total expenditures.

A third consequence of moving up to a larger plateau

as the permanent approach to ministry is reflected in a changing pattern of relationships. In smaller congregations a member's primary group can be the congregation that includes 15 to 40 at worship on Sunday morning. When attendance averages 140 or 230 or 320 or 410, that Sunday morning crowd is too large to function as a primary group. People have to find their friendship circle elsewhere in the life and ministry of that parish. One answer is the group life.

A different facet of that same issue of relationships can be summarized in the question "Who is my pastor?" In the congregation in which the minister is the only full-time person on the payroll, the answer usually is either the current pastor or a beloved predecessor. In the large and rapidly growing congregation, one member turns to the senior minister as "my pastor," another looks to the associate minister, a third will see that relationship with a program specialist, a fourth may identify the church secretary, and a fifth perceives the staff as "a bunch of task-oriented professionals" and turns to a volunteer for pastoral care.

Another common consequence of the successful implementation of a growth strategy is reflected by three criticisms and one affirmative comment. The affirmative comment usually refers to the rise in the level of quality, the increase in the range of choices, and the influx of new people.

The three common criticisms can be summarized by these three frequently heard statements: "I think we've become too professional"; "I used to know everyone, now I don't know anybody"; "We've been growing so fast I can't keep up with everything that's going on around here."

The common thread through all three comments is a

reflection of individual values. One of the cohesive forces in most congregations on a plateau in size is the perception of a common value system. That may not be an accurate reflection of reality. It is perceived to be true because most of the time people are careful not to affirm a discordant value. As the size of the congregation increases, the differences in the value systems among the people become more visible. This is accentuated by newcomers who are pleased their religious needs are being met, but who care little about the deeply held cultural values of the longtime members. Substantial differences in values also exist between older and younger generations in regard to a variety of issues, including marriage, divorce, patriotism, abortion, music, homosexuality, money, war, the work ethic, race, instant gratification, and the role of women in our society.

The more narrowly, precisely, and clearly the theological stance of a congregation is defined, the less likely divisive conflicts over cultural values will arise between longtime members and newcomers or between generations of members. The broader that theological umbrella over a congregation, the more likely these divisive conflicts will emerge as the size of the congregation goes up. This is one factor in a larger explanation of why theologically conservative congregations find it easier to move up off that plateau in size than do the theologically more diverse churches.

Finally, and for some longtime volunteer leaders this is the most unacceptable consequence, growth in numbers often is accompanied by a shift in authority patterns. The basic generalization is the smaller the size of the congregation, the more likely most of the authority will be vested in volunteers. By contrast, in large, and especially in very large and rapidly growing, churches most of the real power rests with the senior pastor and the staff. In small congregations one pattern often is reinforced by the combination of short pastorates and long tenure for the volunteer leaders. The central part of the explanation for this difference is not doctrine or polity. It is knowledge. In Western society knowledge is the chief source of power. In the tradition-bound and past-oriented small congregation, knowledge about the past and local traditions plus long tenure as a volunteer plus a role in the local grapevine as both a sender and a recipient of oral messages plus crucial friendship and kinship ties plus an investment of four or five or six hours of time a week can make one a powerful leader.

In the large and rapidly growing church, knowledge about contemporary reality, an understanding of the goals for the next few years, competence in gathering crucial data from printed sources, and the investment of fifty or sixty hours of time every week are the best sources of knowledge. Since growth means change, long tenure and a deep acquaintance with the past may be a handicap, not an asset in the large and rapidly growing parish.

A second source of this conflict may lie in the distinction between authority and power. The polity of that religious tradition and/or the constitution of that parish may assign a large quantity of authority to the volunteer leaders. The size, complexity, and rapid growth of that parish, however, mean most of the knowledge about contemporary reality is in the heads of staff, even though their legitimate authority is severely limited. The natural and predictable result is frequent clashes between volunteer leaders, who declare they have great authority, and the staff, who derive their power from a huge investment of time, skill, and energy that makes them highly knowl-edgeable leaders. Sometimes this conflict is resolved by the stormy departure of a couple of volunteer leaders. Occasionally it leads to the dismissal of the pastor, who may leave to organize a new congregation. More often, a compromise is worked out that immobilizes all decision makers, and a high degree of passivity is followed by a decline in numbers.

The product of these generalizations is that implemen-tation of a strategy to move up off a plateau in size usually is accompanied by a shift in power from volunteer leaders to paid staff. This is less of a problem in Roman Catholic, Methodist, and Episcopal or Anglican traditions than it is in the Reformed Church in America, the Christian Reformed Church, a couple of the denominations that trace their heritage back to the Anabaptist movement, the Churches of Christ (non-instrumental), and similar traditions that grant great authority to lay elders.

Success can bring unhappy surprises, but that can be a worthwhile trade off!

NOTES

Introduction

1. These views on new church development have been presented in an earlier volume in this series, Lyle E. Schaller, *44 Questions for Church Planters* (Nashville: Abingdon Press, 1991).

1. Why? And Why Not?

1. The meaning and importance of personal stability zones in the lives of people is discussed in Alvin Toffler, *Future Shock* (New York: Random House, 1970), pp. 324-29.
2. The characteristics of the six most common plateaus in size among Protestant churches in North America are discussed in greater detail in Lyle E. Schaller, *Looking in the Mirror* (Nashville: Abingdon Press, 1984), pp. 14-37.
3. This "awkward size church" plateau is analyzed in more detail in Lyle E. Schaller, *The Middle-Sized Church* (Nashville: Abingdon Press, 1985), pp. 99-137.
4. The emergence of the big program church is described in Lyle E. Schaller, *The Seven-Day-A-Week Church* (Nashville: Abingdon Press, 1992).
5. For a provocative discussion on how to move beyond ten thousand at worship, see Carl George, *Prepare Your Church for the Future: Introducing the Mega-Church Model* (Tarrytown, N.Y.: Revell, 1991).
6. For one of the definitive studies of this pattern, see C. Kirk Hadaway, *Growing Off the Plateau* (Nashville: Sunday School Board of the Southern Baptist Convention, 1989). This study reported that 70 percent of all Southern Baptist congregations more than five years old at that time were either on a plateau in size or declining in numbers. Similar studies from other denominations suggest the range is between 65 and 85 percent for American Protestantism.
7. James MacGregor Burns, *Leadership* (New York: Harper & Row, 1978).
8. See Carl S. Dudley, *Making the Small Church Effective* (Nashville: Abingdon Press, 1979) for a superb defense of this role for the pastor of a small church.

2. Act Your Size!

1. The issue of a weak or low congregational self-image is described in Lyle E. Schaller, *Hey, That's Our Church!* (Nashville: Abingdon Press, 1975), pp. 178-92.

3. Read the Warning Signs!

1. One book that can be used for congregational self-appraisal is Schaller, *Looking in the Mirror*.

4. Quality, Responsiveness, and Productivity

1. A more extensive discussion of this point can be found in Lyle E. Schaller, *44 Ways to Increase Church Attendance* (Nashville: Abingdon Press, 1988).

5. Are You Willing to Pay the Price?

1. See Charles Leroux, "At 50, pals of old become an odd couple." *Chicago Tribune*, Tempo Section, August 30, 1991.
2. A remarkably lucid, challenging, and successful case study of the need to pay the price of change is Michael J. Cassara, "Rejuvenating the Smaller Church," *Net Results*, August 1991, pp. 1-2.

6. Visionary Initiating Leadership May Be the Key

1. For a more extended discussion of leadership and planned change, see Burns, *Leadership*; Thomas J. Peters and Robert H. Waterman, Jr., *In Search of Excellence* (New York: Harper & Row, 1982); Judith Hicks Stiehm, *Bring Me Men and Women* (Los Angeles: University of California Press, 1981); John W. Gardner, *On Leadership* (New York: The Free Press, 1990); Lyle E. Schaller, *Getting Things Done* (Nashville: Abingdon Press, 1986); Warren Bennis and Burt Nanus, *Leaders* (New York: Harper & Row, 1985); Aaron Wildavsky, *The Nursing Father: Moses as a Political Leader* (University, Ala.: The University of Alabama Press, 1984).
2. An introduction to the teaching church concept can be found in Schaller, *The Seven-Day-A-Week Church*, pp. 29-37.
3. One example of this is described in Lyle E. Schaller, *Create Your Own Future* (Nashville: Abingdon Press, 1991), pp. 79-80.
4. The role of the long-range planning committee, criteria for selecting the members, and alternative courses of action are described in Schaller, *Create Your Own Future!*
5. A fascinating account of the adversarial relationship between the graduate student and the major professor can be found in James Rhein, "Bad Blood in Academia," *Isthmus of Madison* (Wisconsin) 9, 26 (June 29–July 5, 1984): 8-11.
6. Suggestions for creating a good match can be found in the first four chapters of Lyle E. Schaller, *The Pastor and the People* (Nashville: Abingdon Press, 1986).
7. A description of the relocation process can be found in Lyle E. Schaller, *Choices for Churches* (Nashville: Abingdon Press, 1990), pp. 97-121.
8. See Schaller, *44 Ways to Increase Church Attendance.*
9. See James D. Glasse, *Putting It Together in the Parish* (Nashville: Abingdon Press, 1972), pp. 55-56.

7. Sharpen the Focus!

1. Suggestions for a long-range planning committee can be found in Schaller, *Create Your Own Future!*

8. What Do We Do Next?

1. Relocation is discussed in greater detail in Schaller, *Choices for Churches*, pp. 97-121.
2. Factors to be considered in revising the Sunday morning schedule are discussed in

Lyle E. Schaller, *44 Ways to Expand the Teaching Ministry of Your Church* (Nashville: Abingdon Press, 1992).

3. These and other approaches to ministry are discussed in greater detail in Schaller, *Choices for Churches*, pp. 19-57.

4. See Schaller, *Create Your Own Future!* pp. 17-47.

5. For the contrast between small group dynamics and the unifying principles in large groups, see Lyle E. Schaller, *Effective Church Planning* (Nashville: Abingdon Press, 1979), pp. 17-63.

6. See Lyle E. Schaller, *Activating the Passive Church* (Nashville: Abingdon Press, 1981).

9. When and How Do We Invite?

1. A useful book on direct mail evangelism is Walter Mueller, *Direct Mail Ministry* (Nashville: Abingdon Press, 1989).

2. An exceptionally wise response to the question about the religious needs of people today has been provided by George Gallup, Jr. He has identified six: (1) the need to believe that life is meaningful and has a purpose, (2) the need for a sense of community and deeper relationships, (3) the need to be appreciated and respected, (4) the need to be listened to and to be convinced one is being heard, (5) the need to feel one is growing in the faith, and (6) the need for relevant and practical help in developing a mature faith. George Gallup, Jr., "The Spiritual Needs of Americans Today," *Fellowship in Prayer*, August 1991, pp. 31-36.

10. Four Radical Changes

1. This evolution is described in Schaller, *The Seven-Day-A-Week Church*. The first chapter of that book also describes a contextual change. This is the gradual retreat of denominational structures from the dominant role they filled as recently as the 1950s. In contemporary America the denominational structures gradually are being replaced by parachurch organizations, megachurches, and ad hoc coalitions of congregations. One of the newest examples of an interchurch coalition formed around a single unifying goal is Churches Uniting in Global Missions. This alliance has brought together leaders from more than two dozen different traditions, including liberal, charismatic, evangelical, independent, and middle-of-the-road theological positions.

2. See Schaller, *Looking in the Mirror*, pp. 14-37.

3. Suggestions on this subject can be found in Lyle E. Schaller, *44 Ways to Revitalize the Women's Organization* (Nashville: Abingdon Press, 1990).

11. Growing with Growth

1. See Lyle E. Schaller, *Assimilating New Members* (Nashville: Abingdon Press, 1978).

2. The best single source for a broad range of printed resources for pastors is The Alban Institute, 4125 Nebraska Avenue, N.W., Washington, D.C. 20016. The best single source for resources on evangelism and church growth is the National Evangelistic Association, 5001 Avenue N, Lubbock, TX 79412-2917.